Advance Praise for Live Free

Live Free: The Inner Journey to Healing leads readers on a wonderful journey of spiritual self-discovery, healing, and freedom. With practical, reader-friendly tools and strategies, Gayle Belanger helps readers discover their "True Self," in order that they might experience total and complete freedom. Many lives will benefit from the wisdom found between the pages of this book.

> David Patterson, Lead Pastor
> The Father's House, Vacaville, Calif.

This book, along with Gayle Belanger's teaching and council have not only been critical in rescuing my marriage, but in literally saving my life and securing a legacy of healing that my children and generations after them will inherit. I was trapped in anxiety, depression, and addiction that were destroying my marriage, my family and my life. The concepts she explores and teaches in this book changed everything. Gayle is a spiritual midwife who has delivered us this work birthed out of decades of labor in the fields of human desperation. As Christians, we are taught Christ is the answer, but we are often left confused, desperate, and exposed when crises come to us and all of the "right answers" don't seem to work. Gayle walks us through, so practically, *how* we can appropriate the full measure of Christ's healing love in our lives. Her work synthesizes the entire, essential, and beautiful diversity of scripture, theology, ancient Christian disciplines, philosophy, psychiatry, neuroscience and then distills it all into simple healing intimacy with the Lord that is accessible to everyone. Absolutely solid!

> G. Blake McLaughlin, D.O.
> University of Colorado

Gayle Belanger blesses us with a clear yet profound understanding of how the Holy Spirit that dwells in our heart can first heal us and then equip us to heal others. Simple, eloquent, and scripturally sound, this book is an anointed guide to finding one's fullness in Christ and helping others to do the same. Highly recommended for those trying to help themselves and others heal and reach their full potential in Christ.

> Alan Werblin, M.D.
> Former Chief of Medicine and Medicine/Psychiatry Liaison at Kaiser
> Vacaville, Calif.

I am so inspired by this work taking flight! What Gayle so brilliantly addresses is how to live so completely loved by God when we are aware of our failures and shortcomings. This isn't a concept, but rather a practice that will draw Jesus closer than ever into our daily lives and allow His love and compassion to heal us and be expressed through us into the lives of others. She makes the first two commandments come alive.

Terces Engelhart
Founder, Cafe Gratitude and Gracias Madre
author of *Sacred Commerce* and speaker

Gayle has written a masterful work that explains what it is to be rooted and grounded in love as Eph. 3:17 commands us. She explains the simple process to freedom of self through a Christian meditation like the patriarchs, Jesus and apostles experienced. She guides and encourages the reader in a simple process to discover and become a "True Christian Person." What is the key to freedom? Love! *Live Free: The Inner Journey to Healing* by Gayle Belanger is not just a book on how to experience and how to be set free to love from the inside out, starting with loving yourself and understanding God's love for you. It is also a book of experiences. It was born out of personal experience and then watching as she has guided countless others through the process so they can also live free. We all need to experience the freedom of authentic, abiding, life changing, love. Gayle gives us wonderful guidance in that Journey.

Dennis R. Madden
author of *The Golden Rule of Love: the Measure of Every Thing*
Licensed Professional Counselor, Dallas, TX

Live Free: The Inner Journey To Healing by Gayle Belanger is for everyone. We all have woundings that we have received as children or adults. Remember Junior High? Gayle explains how these affect our daily lives in negative ways. For some, major problems have resulted and there are 12 Step and Group Programs as well as Professional Counselors that provide help. Most of us will not attend such programs because we believe our wounds are insignificant. Gayle explains how anyone can meet with our Lord and receive our healing. In the process, a gift that was nullified is restored and we can be the people God intended for us to be. Jesus is returning for a bride that is pure. We all need this book and the practical approach that is available to everyone everywhere.

Robert Elm, author of *Proverbs for Marriage*
co-author, *Your Marriage as God Imagined*

Live Free: The Inner Journey to Healing is a must-have for every Christ follower! My mind used to be my own worse enemy, controlled by fear of rejection. I'm incredibly thankful for the passion and deep desire God has given Gayle Belanger to help draw others into a close intimate relationship with God through the love and compassion of Jesus. Her teachings, based on God's word, have taught me to love myself, as God has created me. I used to dislike people and tried to avoid them at all cost, but now I look forward to fellowship and building relationships, not just acquaintances.

Rebecca Duvall,
author of *In His Way* and speaker

Live Free

The Inner Journey to Healing

Live Free

The Inner Journey to Healing

Gayle Belanger

with Noelle Locke

This book contains advice and information relating to your emotional and physical state of being. The publisher and author disclaim liability for any negative outcomes that may occur as a result of applying the methods suggested in this book. All identifying details, including names have been changed or omitted except for those that pertain to the author's family members. This book is not intended as a substitute for advice from a trained professional.

To contact the author, please visit livefreeministry.org.

Unless otherwise noted, Scripture quotations are taken from THE NEW KING JAMES VERSION. © 1982 by Thomas Nelson Inc. Used by permission. All rights reserved.

Scripture quotations marked MSG are taken from *The Message*. Copyright © 1993, 1994, 1995, 1996, 2000, 2001, 2002. Used by permission of NavPress Publishing Group.

Scripture quotations marked AMP are taken from THE AMPLIFIED BIBLE. ©1954, 1958, 1962, 1964, 1965, 1987 by the Lockman Foundation (used by permission). All rights reserved.

Scripture quotations marked NLT are taken from the Holy Bible, New Living Translation, copyright© 1996, 2004, 2007 by Tyndale House Foundation. Used by permission of Tyndale House Publishers, Inc., Carol Stream, Illinois 60188. All rights reserved.

Scripture quotations marked NIV are from HOLY BIBLE: NEW INTERNATIONAL VERSION®, NIV© 1973, 1978, 1984, 2011 by Bi (Sorge 2011) (Scazzero 2006) (Eddy 2001) (Guyon n.d.) (J. Guyon n.d.) (Leaf 2007) (Leaf, Switch on your brain: The key to peak happiness, thinking and health. 2013) (Avila 1961)blica, Inc. Used by permission. All rights reserved worldwide.

Scripture quotations marked TPT are taken from *Letters from Heaven by the Apostle Paul*, The Passion Translation ®, copyright © 2014. Used by permission of BroadStreet Publishing Group, LLC, Racine, Wisconsin, USA. All rights reserved.

Scripture quotations marked TPT are taken from *Romans: Grace and Glory*, The Passion Translation ®, copyright © 2015. Used by permission of BroadStreet Publishing Group, LLC, Racine, Wisconsin, USA. All rights reserved.

Scripture quotations marked TPT are taken from *Luke and Acts: To the Lovers of God*, The Passion Translation ®, copyright © 2014. Used by permission of BroadStreet Publishing Group, LLC, Racine, Wisconsin, USA. All rights reserved.

Scripture quotations marked TPT are taken from *1 & 2 Corinthians: Love and Truth*, The Passion Translation ®, copyright © 2014, 2015. Used by permission of BroadStreet Publishing Group, LLC, Racine, Wisconsin, USA. All rights reserved.

Printed by CreateSpace.

Cover design: Kevin Ohlin
Interior design: Noelle Locke

Printed in the United States of America
ISBN-10: 1537288172
ISBN-13: 978-1537288178

To my husband, Frany, who has always supported me in what God has called me to do. Thank you for your patience and love—and sometimes, taking a second place to my work. I love you and could not have done this without you.

To my kids, who loved me through the good times and the hard times; I love you and am grateful to you more than you know.

And to those who are looking for hope and freedom and have not yet found it, this is for you.

Contents

Acknowledgements

First of all, I want to thank all of you who will read this book. This was written for the captives, the brokenhearted and those who desire freedom from their past. I feel honored to be able to share the insights God gave me years ago of this love-journey with Jesus.

I want to thank the many people who encouraged and helped me along the way; Bob Elm, you have stayed by my side believing this should be printed for the public and convincing me to keep going in my many of times of discouragement. Thank you for all the hours of proofreading you have poured into this and for all your Holy Spirit wisdom.

Noelle Locke, you are a Godsend! You came in and completely captured my voice—so much so that you not only helped edit, but write and communicate my heart behind this project. What an amazingly gifted person you are. Most of all, I want to thank you for knowing my heart. It's because you have the same heart for Jesus and you also believe so strongly in the vision the Lord has given me. You are a beautiful woman of God.

I want to thank my whole Live Free volunteer team and my dear friends who have stood with me together in this journey for four years, even when we didn't know where we were going. You all believe in the vision and that it is God's call. You are amazing friends and co-laborers.

Mary McDonald, I appreciate all your help and neuroscience expertise coupled with your supreme knowledge for the written word. You made sure my facts were correct and helped me say so simply what took you many years of education in being a neuroscientist to learn. I am forever grateful for you.

I want to thank The Father's House for trusting me to go forward with this ministry. I love that we have the same vision to see God's people healed and able to walk in the freedom to which they have been called. I thank you from the bottom of my heart. It is for such a time as this.

Tim and Robyn Bittle, you are amazing pastors who believe in this journey and have supported me wholeheartedly. I am eternally grateful to you both.

And without all of my clients I've seen over the years, who have been my biggest fans and at the same time my grace growers: you've encouraged me to get this book out and become the best I can be along the way.

Of course, my husband, Frany, who's idea it was originally to allow me to quit my banking career and go back to college to fulfill my God-given destiny in counseling and ministry. None of this would have come to pass without your ongoing love and support.

Forward

During my 18 years as a family physician, I've seen a steady stream of people presented to my office with a myriad of symptoms both physical and psychological. As a physician and a Christian, I've always done my best to engage my patients at the physical, emotional and spiritual level. I've prescribed lots medication for anxiety and depression and sent many, many referrals for traditional psychotherapy.

For patients with a faith background, I've directed them to their churches, their pastors and to prayer. For those who were open, I prayed with them for healing in their lives. However, many continued to walk through my doors with a wounded heart that influenced so much of their life and worldview.

I always felt there should be a more effective method to heal a wounded heart that could augment traditional treatments. As a physician with a background in science, it would have to have some basis in neuroscience and psychology. As a Christian, it would have to invite God into the healing experience. Gayle's treatment approach has these aspects woven together. It takes the best of self-help, neuroplasticity science, mindfulness training, and combines them with the presence of the Holy Spirit as the Key Healer in the milieu.

This approach systematically creates rapid healing for psychological trauma that would often take months or years in a more traditional setting with more traditional methods. I have seen real healing and transformation take place for patients in a single setting. Further, her method teaches systematic, repetitive self-compassion and Holy Spirit directed compassion, which creates literal armor for any future insults or stressors. I have been astounded by the results of this work for my patients, friends, family, and myself.

I encourage you to enter this reading with an open mind and heart. It is not just another Christian self-help book. It is instead a guidebook to very a different type of approach to a healing method that could transform your life and those you care about.

– Chris Walker, M.D.
Chair, Chiefs of Adult and Family Medicine
Chief of Adult and Family Medicine-Vacaville

backgrounds and cultures—and we don't always know or understand how our past affects our future. Throughout this book, you'll find clear guidelines for you to navigate this charter toward healing and wholeness.

I have had a number of clients over the years tell me that this work is too hard, that they aren't ready, or they'll just "come back another time." They couldn't face their fears of dealing with the old pain, or it hurt too much to even bother. I would watch them push all of the old pain down, hoping it would never raise its ugly head. Some of these people were friends and family I've personally watched die without dealing with their issues, and it broke my heart knowing they could've had so much more in life. But then there are those who take hold of what I teach, and I see them experience massive transformation and freedom from any and every hurt they've endured. It's remarkable to see the night-and-day difference of how life-giving inner healing can be in someone.

Becoming Christ-like is not a destination; it is a journey to becoming one with Christ. It involves knowing who we are in Christ and being rooted in His love. Paul speaks of it when he mentions being filled "with all the fullness of God" (Eph. 3:19). Jesus prayed to the Father asking on our behalf, "that they also may be one in us" (John 17:21). God's desire is that "we continually be in union with Him, as we are privileged to be in union with Christ, who is in union with God" (1 Cor. 3:23, MSG).

The rewards and promises of God are richer and deeper than anything we can think, ask or imagine this side of heaven. We can be conformed to the image of Jesus—and become more like our loving, joyful, wise, caring and powerful Lord and Savior. My prayer is that as you read this and actively apply it to your life, you will fully come to experience all He has for you while on this Earth. God made this healing freedom available to you by what Jesus has already done at the cross.

Chapter 1

WHY LOVE IS THE KEY

"Love becomes the mark of true maturity." – Colossians 3:14 TPT

Since I was a little girl, I always wanted to be around people and have friends. I went to school with the sole intent to enjoy friendship and love people, not necessarily to study as my first priority. This desire for intimate relationships with others is something I have always longed for, ever since I could remember. When I encountered Jesus at a very young age, I always believed I had a natural connection to His love that somehow, I knew lived within me. Looking back, this seemed a little strange since no one in my family had any real relationship with Jesus or considered themselves "Christian."

Over the years of continuing my simplistic walk with Jesus, things started spiraling out of control in my life, and I considered giving up on everything. One dark

1

night, in the midst my life's chaos, I heard the Lord's voice come to me loud and clear, saying if I gave up, I would miss the reward that was coming in my latter years. This startled me into a completely different thought process: there was a whole journey to loving Jesus that went beyond "I love Jesus, and Jesus loves me."

Soon a continuous nudging in my spirit came to me: "I want you to love greater; there is more for you than this." This spiritual hunger for Jesus was curious and all so new to me, and the dissatisfaction of not having enough of the Lord's love in my spirit continued to intensify. Frustrated in not being able to attain the level of love I desired and felt called to have, this dissatisfaction I carried turned to a burning passion of pursuing the depth of His love, and I prayed it would never die out.

> *Jesus puts the desires in our hearts, and it's His promise to fulfill them.*

I searched His word for revelation to my dilemma and came across Psalms 37:4 (NLT), which says, "Take delight in the Lord and He will give you the desires of your heart." I was powerfully impacted to learn God doesn't only give us the desires of our heart, but He is the one responsible to fulfill them. It was Jesus who originally put the desire to expand His love in me, and it was His promise to fulfill it. This was so powerful to help me understand: it wasn't based on of my effort to fill myself with His love, but God's gracious and merciful ability to pour His love into my heart.

One day in prayer, I asked, "Lord, please fill me with more of You; only You can take me deeper in Your love." God answered and revealed the way to receive that deeper level of His love was to give out the love

> *God's love can completely transform your life into one of total and complete freedom.*

I had to others—and this act would keep my passion for Jesus burning forever. Giving and ministering God's love to others made more room for me to receive God's love on a whole new level—and I realized this beautiful desire would continue growing as I stayed connected to Him. My personal encounter of this newfound love from God launched me into my own journey of healing and freedom, and in turn, became my mission and call to help others live free, just like I was beginning to experience myself.

After 20 years of being on staff as an addiction counselor in a local church, and now having my own ministry healing people to live in their God-given freedom, my desire is to show you how God's love can completely transform your life into one of total and complete freedom.

The inner journey[1] to becoming the person God designed you to be begins here—with first learning to

---

[1] Teresa Avila, "Interior Castle," 1961 was one of the saints of old who first spoke about an inward journey with God.

see God as He *really* is and how He sees you. This is done several ways, but it first starts with understanding God's great love for you. You can only move forward in becoming the person God intends you to be by continually experiencing this deep love He has for you.

The reason we start with the topic of love is because *love is the very core of God.* The Bible says God is love: "Whoever does not love does not know God, because God is love" (1 John 4:8 NIV). Love is not something God simply does; it's actually the character and nature of God. God desires us to realize the tremendous love He has for us, and He also wants us to learn how to love our self the way He sees us, so we can, in turn, also love others.

You may already know that God loves you. But are you able to love others freely? Can you accept where any one person is in his or her own process of growth? Can you do this without judgment or rejection?

A lot of times depression, anxiety or self-criticism (among other things) gets the best of us and it becomes easy to fall into the trap of wondering why anyone would love us in our current condition. I believe we can only love others as much as we love ourselves. When you don't love who you are, or if you can't love who God made you to be, your thoughts and words will be pretty faithful to show you.

Have you ever come across thoughts like, "I'm so stupid; I can't believe I did that"? Or have you caught yourself saying, "I'm such an idiot for saying or thinking (this or that)"? In my years of experience as a counselor, these are clear indicators that help people see there is a part within us all that does not love and embrace our whole self.

4

The Apostle Paul prayed: "that you being rooted and grounded in love, may be able to comprehend with all the saints what is the width and length and depth and height—to know the love of Christ which passes knowledge; that you may be filled with all the fullness of God" (Eph. 3:17-19). This is one of God's goals for us.

With this prayer in mind, ask yourself: how in the world can *I* be filled with all the fullness of God? How do *I* stay rooted and grounded in love? The freedom you will experience from everyday frustrations and pain is directly related to your ability to remain rooted and grounded in love. Just imagine how your life would be if you could continually live out of a solid state of love: no rejection; no hiding; no more running from something or someone who hurt or hurts you; no more suffering through bitterness because someone offended you—however great the offense. Can you picture it? Your default responses would be established out of Christ's love, and your thoughts toward others, including yourself, would be free to love and be kind and compassionate.

This all has to begin with learning to love YOU first. It is impossible to understand the Lord's great love for you until *you* learn to love all of the parts of yourself: the good, the bad and the ugly. One of the basic reasons you may find it difficult to love Jesus or God, or felt you couldn't love Him adequately enough is because you haven't accepted or extended love to yourself. If you have ever found it taxing to extend unconditional love and acceptance to other people with their faults, this too, stems from not loving and accepting your whole self first.

The word of God says, "You shall love the Lord your God with all your heart, with all your soul, with all your mind and with all your strength. This is the first commandment. And the second is like it: You shall love your neighbor as yourself"(Mark 12:30-31). The second commandment in this scripture has an order we often overlook, but when read carefully, I believe God commands us to love ourselves first before we can ever love our neighbor. If this is the case, we can only love our neighbor to the degree we can love ourselves.

> *You can only love yourself as much as you allow God to love you.*

Jesus knew the Father's heart was to have a deep, intimate, love-relationship with His people, so this commandment is dependent on three elements: to love ourselves (who He created us to be), (so that we can) love our neighbor, and receive God's love and love God in return. You can only love God as much as you love yourself. And you can only love yourself as much as you allow God to love you. A way to determine how well you love other people and God is to ask yourself: "How well do I extend love and kindness to myself?"

In my experience with my clients, guilt and shame show up in various forms: I've seen people deny responsibility for their part of an argument; I've heard people judge others without understanding the situation and I've also watched people totally deny their own feelings because they fear being exposed and vulnerable. Maybe it's just the small issues that you tend to dismiss, such as wanting to win, or always be "right," or being selfish or greedy. This is what can make it so hard to accept and love ourselves (and others) as Jesus does.

Jesus wants us to learn how to love ourselves in spite of our humanness and how to have the compassion for others in their humanness. I believe He knew our condition and the shame and guilt we would feel when we mess up or sin, or react to others' shortcomings. The good news is when we do mess up, the power of the cross is meant for your every day freedom and cleansing. As you bring your confessions to Jesus in repentance, He places your sin at the foot of the cross so you can begin again with a clean slate. By doing this as a daily practice, you can continue to walk in His love with freshness and purity and also eliminate any guilt or shame. The word says His mercy is new every morning: "God's loyal love couldn't have run out, His merciful love couldn't have dried up. They're created new every morning. How great is your faithfulness" (Lam. 3:22-23 MSG).

> *Love is not something we are responsible for generating ourselves.*

Love is not something we are responsible for generating ourselves. It does not come *from* us; it comes *to* us from God by way of the Holy Spirit when we believe in Him and His word. Jesus showed the world love so that people could live as God intended (John 16:7). So He fulfilled the law—by loving us first so we can love Him, our self and others out of a response to what He did.

The Holy Spirit—our Teacher and Counselor—helps us to understand and grasp His love as we live out our lives, so that we know it completely in body, soul and spirit. The Bible tells us, "The love of God has been poured out in our hearts by the Holy Spirit who was given to us" (Rom. 5:5). The Holy Spirit loves us so much that He pours the love of God into our hearts so we might know His love, be transformed by it and share that love with others. Remember, this is a lifelong process in which you will participate. It's a journey you take—not a destination for which you strive. This is a daily journey, friend!

Now as a true Christ-follower, I have learned through bible studies and reading about the saints of old that there was a journey of growing in God's love that was supposed to take place, and that it would ultimately lead to divine union with Him.[2] This process of learning and accepting true love begins when you allow Jesus to love you by sitting quietly in His presence. In the next few chapters I will guide you through entering into a new freedom of learning how to love and be loved. It is an exciting journey that will continually keep you running after the abundant life only found in Jesus.

---

[2] Thomas Keating, *Open Mind, Open Heart* 20th ed. (New York: Continuum

Chapter 2

THE TRUE SELF

"Often it's not about becoming a new person but becoming the person you were meant to be, and already are, but don't know how to be."

—Heath L. Buckmaster

As I received my calling from God to love others, I pursued my certification to be an addiction counselor at Bible College. After I started back to school, I realized I really didn't know who I was. It seemed there were so many facets of my personality, but I couldn't discern what was mine, and what I picked up from others. I remember standing at my kitchen sink crying out to God, "Lord, who am I *really?*"

Along my life's journey, I became so dependent on the opinions of others and their ideas of who they thought I should be, that I had to seek recovery from all the emotional co-dependency that resulted from it. Somewhere, I lost myself along the way and in a

> *You now have His divine nature's power to take authority over your old ways.*

moment, it dawned on me: "I don't even know who I am."

Knowing God's love prepares you to step into your true identity in Christ that has been established by His work on the cross; you are now a brand new creation (2 Cor. 5:17). You have been given a new spirit infused with His Holy Spirit, so your true identity has been made perfect, healed and whole. Colossians 3:9-10 (TPT) says:

> Now that you have embraced new creation life as the true reality, lay aside your old Adam-self with its masquerade and disguise. For you have acquired new creation life, which is continually being renewed into the likeness of the One who created you; giving you the full revelation of God.

Your new identity in Christ is not tied to your old ways of thinking and behaving. You now have His divine nature's power to take authority over those old ways. This "new you" is what I refer to as the "True Christian Person," or your "True Self."[3] And it is the basis for your ongoing transformation.

As I began my inner journey, I watched the Lord reveal my True Self piece by piece. This is a process, and you will encounter more of the full picture of the true you as you get to know the Lord more intimately.
In this chapter, I want you to be able to identify with your True Self, so you can begin exploring the deeper

---

[3] Thomas Keating, *Open Mind, Open Heart*, 11.

parts of your life that need attention, healing or greater freedom. To do this, ask yourself:

- ❏ Is there anything in your life that's not working despite your best efforts?
- ❏ Do you feel you've reached your fullest potential?
- ❏ Are you living and doing what you were created to do?

There is a deeper walk with God available for you. Sometimes the deeper parts of our life that need attention have buried themselves so thoroughly that we don't even realize it's a problem.

You may be functioning relatively well at work and with people in your life, but all of us have believed lies at some point. Identifying the truth about yourself and calling out even the seemingly most insignificant lies will lead to a deeper walk with God and a more fulfilling day-to-day life.

Your true identity in Christ is one of the core elements I include in this book on inner healing because it complements the process for Jesus to heal any and all wounds of your heart. You don't have to have a dark or abusive past to qualify for needing healing or a deeper walk with the Lord. Life itself is cruel at times to all of us.

The more you know God's love, the more His Holy Spirit draws you into life-changing

> *Sometimes the deeper parts of our life that need attention have buried themselves so thoroughly that we don't even realize it's a problem.*

unity with Him. As you become assured of His love, you will start to open up and release the hidden and broken pieces of your life. It is important you learn to love the broken pieces and develop your True Self *in a safe environment* that is free from judgment, criticism or negativity. Otherwise, you will be inhibited from fully seeing, understanding and embracing your True Christian Person.

Within the True Christian Person, you will experience great depths of His love and healing, which will translate into increasingly new levels of freedom from toxic and negative thoughts. Remember, these are the thoughts that steal your joy or are sly to deceive you into thinking "you're not enough" or "you're not good enough" for what's in front of you.

HOW TO EMBRACE THE TCP IN YOU

Foundationally having your identity of the True Christian Person empowers you to embrace all of who God made you to be (Rom. 8:17, 2 Pet. 1:3-4). Living life out of this position, you can love yourself, love God, and love His crowned creation, humanity—and this an unshakeable premise.

Your identity isn't based on what you have done, but what Christ did for you that makes it possible to live out your life to the fullest. Although you may know this intellectually, I want you to make it personal and own and embrace it for yourself with "I am Statements."

"I am Statements" are tools I like to use to help you connect and identify who you are in Christ. These statements declare who you truly are according to what Jesus has done for you; they are not statements based on human effort that revolve around how you have

tried to be a "good person" or "good Christian." No—
these are biblically based God-truths that will help you
come against the lies of the enemy and advocate inner
healing.

It's statements such as:

- ◆ I am the temple of God; (1 Cor. 3:16)
- ◆ I am blessed, bestowed upon; (Deut. 28:6)
- ◆ I am chosen, set aside for purpose; (John 15:16)
- ◆ I am holy and without blame; (Eph. 1:4)
- ◆ I am loved, adored; (Eph. 2:4)
- ◆ I am adopted, handpicked; (Rom. 8:15)
- ◆ I am washed, pure; (1 Cor. 6:11)
- ◆ I am fearfully and wonderfully made; (Ps. 139:14)
- ◆ I am accepted, approved, a joint-heir; (Rom. 8:7)
- ◆ I am redeemed, paid for in full; Gal. 3:13
- ◆ I am forgiven and my mistakes (past, present,
  future) are cancelled, acquitted; (Heb. 8:12, Eph.
  1:7)
- ◆ I am anointed, consecrated, chosen and part of a
  royal priesthood; (1 Pet. 2:9)
- ◆ I am partaker of His divine nature. (2 Pet. 1:3-4)

Another way to think of the True Christian Person is to
imagine in your mind what your spirit will look like; it's
the part that someday is going to heaven. If you and I
both died today, how would I be able to identify you in
Heaven among others? Colossians 3:11 (TPT) says,
"In this new creation life, your nationality makes no
difference, or your ethnicity, education, or economic
status—they matter nothing. For it is Christ that means
everything as he lives in every one of us!" Set aside all
your credentials, titles and positions. Put aside your
outward appearance, your marital status or the number
of children you have.

Picture the *real* you, filled with the love, joy, peace, righteousness and the strength of the Lord that His word promises for His children. Imagine being filled with *all* the fullness of God; picture sharing His divine love with others. See yourself with all your wonderful personality traits or characteristics; what makes you *uniquely you.*

This image you can see of yourself—your heavenly spirit personified—is the part that is completely healed and whole. As the True Christian Person, you are free from any issues and hurts; you are physically and emotionally strong and filled with an overwhelming love because you stand in the presence of Jesus! This, my friend, is who you were created to be. And you must embrace and live out of this place to live life delivered from all that weighs you down.

Now it's your turn. I want you to take the time to see what *your* True Self looks like by writing out several "I am statements." Using your sanctified imagination, picture yourself in this way as the True Self God intends. Remember, this is not the place to mention any negative issues about yourself. What does it look and feel like for you? This is not an exhaustive list, but a few examples can include:

- I am a deeply devoted man or woman of God.
- I am fiercely committed to my family.
- I love to serve others, especially in my home or community.
- I am deeply caring towards children and/or animals.
- I easily perceive and feel the emotions of others.
- I am highly creative and artistic and can see things with an unusual perspective.

When I picture my own True Self, some of my "I am statements" include:

- I desire to go after the deep things of God.
- I am a lover of people, especially the broken and hurting.
- I can easily discern the heart of others.
- I love to equip others with God's truths.
- I am curious and always want to learn new things.
- I love to spend time in secluded parts of nature.

Even though it took me a while to absorb what Jesus was showing me, my desire is for you to grasp this picture of who you truly are in Him today. Journal it out onto paper, or save it electronically so you can refer to it when you need it until it becomes an automatic response.

Knowing and being able to see your True Christian Person sets you up to enter into the next part of your inner

Another way to think of the True Christian Person is to imagine in your mind what your spirit will look like; it's the part that someday is going to heaven.

healing. All this works hand in hand with meditation, and as you learn and practice meditating on His word, you will begin to see yourself as Jesus sees you, the True Christian Person, completely transformed. When you take up your cross daily and follow Him, you will encounter a new purpose-driven destiny where God is calling you into freedom.

Chapter 3

SEEKING HIS FACE: MEDITATING ON JESUS

"The amount of time we spend with Jesus—meditating on His word and His majesty, seeking His face—establishes our fruitfulness in the kingdom."
- Charles Stanley

We are at war with the world's ways of living out our destiny. In today's frantic society, the demand for our time and attention can heavily tax our mind to run at a progressively accelerated pace. Our to-do list seems to grow longer with each passing day: school needs your homework assignments; your boss wants more time to finish his important project; your family needs you at home to help with chores, or pick up your kids or make time for date night with your spouse. You name it; the requests for your time and attention are behind every corner. If you give in to all these demands, you will function in a rush that breeds chaos, stress, turmoil and anxiety.

> *Biblical meditation is actually something the Bible requires and commands of every Christ-follower.*

The worldly concept of meditation is something often associated with eastern religions that focus its thinking on nothing specific, or encourage you to empty your mind to transcend out of who you are. But biblical meditation is actually something the Bible requires and commands of every Christ-follower: "If there is any virtue and if there is anything praiseworthy—meditate on these things" (Phil. 4:8b). The same verse in the Passion Translation says it another way: "So keep your thoughts continually fixed [...] and fasten your thoughts on every glorious work of God, praising him always."

There are actually two aspects to biblical meditation that referred to in scripture. Logos—which is the actual word of God that is quoted scripture from the Bible, and Rhema—which is a word given to us from the Holy Spirit in a given moment or situation. They work hand in hand to meditate on the written word of God (logos) and allow the Holy Spirit to use it (rhema) as we change and renew our minds.[4]

My passion as a counselor is to impart truth into others as God has done so clearly for me. Years ago, I worked on staff at my local church as an addiction counselor. At the time, I really felt led by the Holy Spirit to approach the Lead Pastor with a life-changing decision for me and all my clients: to start a new

---

[4] Got Questions Ministries. "What is the rhema word?" August 27, 2016. www.gotquestions.org/rhema-word.html.

ministry based on abiding meditation. It would take the contemplation and deep reflection of the truths of God (meditation) and personally apply it (abiding) to continue healing the wounds of our hearts.

I also began to study and practice Christian meditation after reading and learning from several books expanding on spiritual disciplines. They were directly tied to desiring a deeper connection with Jesus, which I desperately hungered for. This change in direction and new approach in my counseling was the very thing that helped me establish and reflect the true purpose of what God had called me to do in setting the captives free (Luke 4:18).

The leading I got from the Holy Spirit was on point that day. Now, one of the first things I require any of my new clients is they receive and apply the tools of Christian meditation that I teach.

This kind of mediation will allow you to experience intimacy with the Lord that will help you process deep emotional hurts and wounds so you can receive freedom and healing quickly. You will also find and learn how to embrace who you really were born to be and how to live the life God has designed for you here on Earth.

Even though I had only been practicing and studying this kind of meditation for a year or so, nothing before that seemed to heal the core of all my hurts as quickly as this. The practice of Christian meditation I studied and applied was the key that allowed God to change me, and all the people I was working with and counseling. I had new perspective and understanding of who I was in Him as I meditated on Jesus. I noticed the Lord would bring up memories of pivotal times in my life and reveal His healing perspective in these different situations.

Christian meditation is contemplative and deeply reflective on the incredible love and beauty of our infinite God; it's where love rises up to replace our fears.

As the intimate connection with Jesus is strengthened, so is your inner man. Ephesians 3:16 gives us a basis to stand on solid ground and not just escape fear, but actually overcome it, "that He would grant you, according to the riches of His glory, to be strengthened with might by His Spirit in the inner man."

In this way we die to the leading of our own independent soul (the thoughts in our mind that rise up and try to take over) and instead, live by the Holy Spirit's leading.

> *The Lord will bring up memories of pivotal times in your life and reveal His healing perspective in these different situations.*

People who desire true freedom will be ready for intimacy with the Lord and the accelerated healing only God can do. Of course, you have to take the time to sit with Him in order to have this closeness with God.

Figure 3.1 is a comparison between two types of meditation that will help reveal the differences, and how critical abiding meditation affects your walk with Jesus.

Figure 3.1[5]

MEDITATION:	Christian	Eastern
GOAL:	Attempts to empty ourselves of false thinking; a time allowed to be filled by God	Attempts to empty the mind; reach a place of nothingness
DETACHES FROM:	Demands of our culture	The world in order to escape the misery of existence
LEADS TO:	Inner healing and wholeness to give ourselves freely to God	Loss of personhood, individuality to merge with cosmic mind
THE EXPERIENCE:	A divine human encounter where we rest in Christ who loves us	Confined to a totally human experience
GOD IS:	Yahweh; the personal Creator	The evocative other
STANDARD OF TRUTH:	The Bible	Evolving and eclectic
JESUS IS:	The Son of God	An enlightened teacher
WAY OF SALVATION:	Purchased by Jesus' blood	No such thing
FOCUS:	Christ	Man
CONCERN:	Divine love	Awareness
HOW:	Faith-based relationship accessible to a living, personal God	Simple relaxation exercise with breathing techniques
WISDOM:	God's	Man's
POWER:	Through Christ	Through man
NEXT STAGE:	Brought about by God	Brought about by man
STANCE:	Man receiving from God to become more Christ-like	Man reaching to become god

[5] James W. Goll, *The Lost Art of Practicing His Presence* (Destiny Image Christian Publishers: 2006).

The only answer is to stay centered in the peace of God who resides within you; to be still—to quiet a racing mind and a fast-paced life. I like to refer to this as getting centered.

God calls us to meditate on His word and be still: "This book of the Law shall not depart from your mouth, but you shall meditate on it day and night, that you may observe to do according to all that is written in it" (Josh. 1:8a). It is again commanded in the book of Psalms: "Be still, and know that I am God; I will be exalted among the nations, I will be exalted in the earth!" (Ps. 46:10). How many of us actually know how to meditate on the word of God day and night, much less, know how to "be still"?

To get to that place where we are centered in our spirit as the True Christian Person with Jesus, we need to move from our head to our heart—transitioning the head knowledge in our mind, to engaging our inner man or woman. Entering into His presence is really a refocusing of our awareness. Rather than being focused on the mind's chatter and fear-based thoughts in our heads, our awareness becomes tuned to the thoughts of God. This allows the essence of God in our spirit to flow into the soul (mind, will and emotions) until our whole person is full with God.

PREPARING YOUR OWN SPACE

In order for your inner man or woman to commune with God, you must intentionally prepare yourself and your surroundings.

First, find a favorite place that is quiet and free from distractions. It is of utmost importance that you take time each day to commune in a beautiful, peaceful and loving space (location) with your Lord. Preferably, the same place each time. I find the anointing of His Spirit builds up in that spot and it become a sacred place. As you make this your daily routine, you will find the Lord waiting there for you.

> *You need to move from your head to your heart to get to the place where you are centered with Jesus.*

Next, still your body and your mind. Since you want to hear His "still, small voice," (1 Kings 19:12, 13) you must not only learn how to quiet your mind, but also how to quiet your body's nervous system. I find listening to some worship music, having a cup of tea or coffee, or just sitting for a couple of minutes, letting your heart rate slow down helps. It is very difficult to enter the Lord's presence with our bodies agitated and tense.

PREPARING TO ENTER INTO YOUR SECRET ROOM

Christian meditation is not specifically a time for "prayer" as you may traditionally think of it. Although asking God for things and petitioning Him on behalf of others is important, this is not the place, nor is this a time of seeking His leading as to what path to take or choice to make.

> *God's word flows from His spirit into your spirit. Then from your spirit, it transforms your mind.*

This is purely a time of worship. It is to be a loving, positive time full of giving thanks, praise and gratitude; a time where you learn how to develop a continuing loving relationship with Him.

It is also not designated to study the Scripture. Trying to force your mind by studying or memorizing the Bible is not the same as reading the word to allow it to permeate you. You want to let it go deep and inspire you from within. God's word flows from His Spirit into your spirit. Then from your spirit, it transforms your mind.

The purpose of this time is to draw near to God and enjoy His presence. As you move deeper into His presence, keep your spirit concentrated on His word so your mind remains aligned with Him.

When you do your meditation, it is critical that you begin with your True Christian Person in your mind's eye. I have seen time and time again those who do not do this as a daily discipline, and I watch people slowly slip into an old identity that is nothing close to what God intended for them.

A young female friend of mine has started to understand and believe, "Wow, I do have value and am truly loved," and has experienced how the Lord sees her as she meditates on her true identity in Christ. But when she stops meditating on her True Self day to day, I see the same young woman who experienced such a close connection with Jesus be so easily offended in a moment.

If a family member insults their son or brother about his inabilities to not quite "measure up," he has two choices; he can be offended and hold it against his wrongdoer, or he can rest confidently in God's ability to take care of him in that situation—and others to come. If you practice meditating as your True Christian Person every day (and throughout the day), you will not be so easily prone to offense.

In the case of the family's son or brother, you would be able to identify it was *the family member's insecurity* that accused him in the first place. You will even be able to extend compassion and forgiveness toward the vilest offenders in your life when you do your meditation. Seriously, friend, make this a constant, *daily* discipline in your life!

Picturing your True Christian Person will help you see yourself as Christ sees you. Later as you begin inner healing, it will keep you grounded and centered to protect you from reliving any bad memories.

ENTER INTO THE SECRET PLACE

My meditation time often follows a pattern of sorts—but there is a method behind my madness. This process of steps that I've outlined below is designed to help take you from your head to your heart.

I call this the "secret place"[6] as referred to in the scripture: "But you, when you pray, go into your room, and when you have shut your door, pray to your Father who is in the secret place; and your Father who sees in secret will reward you openly" (Matt. 6:6).

Since there is no proper or perfect way to meditate, you can adjust this to fit you and your needs. This system I've outlined below is still an invaluable tool that I want

---

[6] Bob Sorge, *Secrets of the Secret Place,* (Grandview: Oasis House, 2011), 4.

you to be equipped with to make your meditation time with the Lord most fruitful. Let's begin!

CREATE A SPACE free from distractions and commotion. Silence or turn off your cell phone if you have to. You don't have to be sitting; walking in a peaceful location also works. Find and make a space free from interruptions—whatever that looks like for you.

FIND A COMFORTABLE POSITION—but not so comfortable that you fall asleep! I have found that lying down really doesn't work well.

CLOSE YOUR EYES AND BE SILENT as your body settles. Picture your True Christian Person at this point in time. *Do not move deeper into meditation until you have a good grasp of your True Self envisioned.*

FOCUS ON BREATHING in the breath of God; with each breath, breathe in His presence, His peace and His love. Exhale all that is not of Him, letting go of all those toxic thoughts and emotions.

ASK THE HOLY SPIRIT to inspire you with a sacred word or song. (Often I focus on the name of Jesus because it is the name above all names.) *Holy One, Lamb of God, King of Kings*, the *Alpha and Omega* and *the Great I AM* are other names that can be used, too. You may find it helpful to focus on a Scripture you have selected beforehand.

NOW, PICTURE YOUR TRUE CHRISTIAN PERSON standing at the top of a flight of stairs. This is the same True Christian Person you already identified in your "I am Statements" in the chapter

26

before. With your True Self in mind, imagine the flight of stairs leading from your mind down to your heart where Jesus dwells. Picture Jesus standing beside you as He leads you down the stairs into this secret place. This is not a dark, scary place, but a beautiful and safe place.

WITH EACH STEP, feel yourself surrendering deeper and deeper into His will, becoming more at peace trusting Him beside you. Allow Jesus' presence to remove any fears or apprehension. Continue down while releasing the daily tension and allowing your body to relax.

AS YOU REACH THE BOTTOM of the stairs, picture a set of gates before you. As you thank Jesus, picture the gates being opened up for you. Praise Him as you enter His courts. (Ps. 100:4)

WALK ACROSS AND DOWN a beautiful courtyard and come to the door of the secret place. This is a sacred place devoted to God's Holy presence; it's the Holy of Holies. There is no sickness, no sadness and no sin here. As you pass through and open the door, this is an important access point, as you have been given free access to the Holy of Holies. He opens the door for you to usher you inside. (Matt. 7:7-8)

CLOSE THE DOOR BEHIND YOU. This represents keeping out the distractions and worries of the day—and anything not of the Lord. (Matt. 6:6)

AS YOU ENTER into the secret place, picture a communion table set *just for you and your Lord.* Allow your table to be a joyful place; a place you feel comfortable and safe; a place set up just for you to share your heart and be transparent with Jesus. This is a time to give Him all of you. Let Him have complete access and recall...*"not my will, but yours be done"* (Luke 22:42b NIV).

IN HIS PRESENCE, worship Him with heartfelt thoughts of love and adoration. Speak to your Lord in secret, creating a private heart-to-heart conversation between you and God. Let more than words—let feelings and thoughts too deep for words—flow into your communication. Use your favorite Scriptures to worship and adore Him here. This will help you imagine being one with Him, the one you adore. During this time I have also found it beneficial to surrender your worries, fears and anxiety over to Jesus (John 17:21, 1 Cor. 6:17).

PAUSE FREQUENTLY and soak in the deep intimacy you are experiencing. In full surrender, let Jesus awaken your heart and flood through all the caverns of your soul. Allow His glory to invade your whole being.

AT THE END of the meditation time, remain silent, eyes closed for a few minutes. Allow yourself to soak in the presence of the Lord. Let His goodness permeate every part of you.

Spending at least 20 minutes with the Lord in the morning and 20 minutes in the late afternoon or evening is what I recommend.[7] It has become a routine I treasure and have found I cannot live without. It is a key that unlocks His power in my life, and it will for you too, friend.

---

[7] Thomas Keating, *Open Mind, Open Heart*, 23.

This will help you to stay centered in Christ all day and to continually walk in His love while fulfilling God's command to meditate on His word day and night.

It is normal if your mind becomes distracted by other presiding thoughts from your day. Don't be hard on yourself when your mind wanders. Simply refocus by returning over and over again to that peaceful place in God's presence. Oppose any inner dialogue with yourself and all wandering thoughts by gently bringing your focus back to Jesus. In this way, you retrain your mind that it does not get to rule over your spirit man.

This will take practice. In the beginning it may not seem possible to fellowship with God in this way, but this is how we were created to live our lives.

Our Ego—the inner critic—can tell us that we aren't accomplishing anything and it feels like a waste of time. This is what the carnal mind wants us to believe, "because the carnal mind is enmity against God" (Rom. 8:7). Since we are a people who always desire to be "doing" something, this can be a very difficult mental battle. With time, you will come to relish resting and abiding in Jesus so much so that your communion with Him becomes a constant way of life.

> *Our Ego (the inner critic) can tell us that we aren't accomplishing anything and that it feels like a waste of time.*

Christian meditation is *vital* to the renewing of your mind. I have found it to be such a basic key in healing our thought lives, which is foundational when we are trying to change our behaviors: "Stop imitating the ideals and opinions of the culture around you, but be inwardly transformed by the Holy Spirit through a total reformation of how you think. This will empower you to discern God's will as you live a beautiful life, satisfying and perfect in his eyes" (Rom. 12:2 TPT).

Chapter 4

EDGING GOD OUT: THE FALSE SELF

"Above all the grace and the gifts that Christ gives to His beloved is that of overcoming self." – St. Francis of Assisi

When I was working through all my emotional baggage, I found a part of me that wanted to overpower my loving True Self with anger and control. I had always hated this part of me, and I didn't want to face that this angry girl within was the real me that God created.

In order to live out of the position of the True Christian Person, it is necessary to understand there is also a False Self competing for power within us.[8] The Bible describes the False Self as your flesh; your Ego;

---

[8] Thomas Keating, *Invitation to Love: The Way of Christian Contemplation,* (New York: The Continuum Publishing Company, 1998), 14-18.

its the carnal man and unwelcome intruder of sin in all of us (Rom. 7:17 TPT, Gal. 2:20 MSG). It revolves around external things such as reputation, job, status, ministry, family or health as its own god, instead of Jesus Christ as Lord. This False Self is the part that is separate from God and what acts out independently from Him. It is what *edges God out* of a person's life when it takes control over the spirit man. Your Ego is driven and defined by its independence and self-reliance, and consequently, this is where most decisions are made outside of God's desire for your best.[9]

> *Your Ego is what edges God out of your life when it takes control over your spirit man.*

Scripture tells us we are a triune being—spirit, soul, and body— and the order of these three components within us actually matters (1 Thess. 5:23). As a child of God, you are to be aligned with your spirit in control—not your soul or body calling the shots. Romans 8:5-6 (TPT) says: "Those who are motivated by the flesh only pursue what benefits themselves. But those who live by the impulses of the Holy Spirit are motivated to pursue spiritual realities. For the mindset of the flesh is death, but the mindset controlled by the Spirit finds life and peace."

You live with your spirit in control when you live out of your True Self. But if your soul or body is in charge, then you live out of the False Self. Ever wonder why you don't understand when you want to do what is right, but can't seem to? So did the apostle Paul in the

---

[9] Watchman Nee, *The Spiritual Man,* vol. 1 (New York: Christian Fellowship Publishers, Inc, 1968), 109-114.

Bible. In Romans 7:15 (AMP) he says, "For I do not understand my own actions [I am baffled and bewildered by them]. I do not practice what I want to do, but I am doing the very thing I hate [and yielding to my human nature, my worldliness—my sinful capacity]." We can have a better understanding of our inner conflict, just like Paul did, as we become aware of the False Self leading us instead of the Holy Spirit being in control. Each of these components will help you understand the role it plays as you live out who you are in Christ and how the False Self can interfere.

SPIRIT

Think of an apple. At its core, you have the seeds, then the actual fruit, then the skin. The core—the very thing that contains the seed within is like our spirit. God designed our *spirit* to be the seat of our intuition, conscience and communion with God.[10] Our spirit holds God's life and communes with Him. When we accept Jesus, God sends His Holy Spirit to live in our spirit. Ezekiel 36:26 says, "I will give you a new heart and put a new spirit within you." John 3:6 tells us, "That which is born of the Spirit is spirit." God's intent is that the Holy Spirit in us would saturate our soul and body with Himself. Starting from the spirit, which is the deepest core of ourselves, Christ is formed in us.

> *God's intent is that the Holy Spirit in you would saturate your soul and body with Himself.*

When you lead your life with your spirit man (or woman) in control, you have formed the perfect alignment with your Lord.

---

[10] Ibid., vol. 2, 93.

33

Otherwise, your False Self can highjack your freedom from being one with Christ. "So if left to myself, the flesh is aligned with the law of sin, but now my renewed mind is fixed on and submitted to God's righteous principles" (Rom. 7:25b TPT). This is a place of victory over sin patterns, with love and protection from outside forces of darkness, because your mind, will and emotions submit to His Holy Spirit within you. Divine union occurs when we live out of this place with the spirit leading over soul and body.

SOUL[11]

God designed the *soul* to be the seat of your mind, will and emotions. Your soul is your personality and the framework that holds your thought processes, your desires and your feelings. Your soul determines how you think, feel and behave toward God, yourself and others. The Holy Spirit within you passes through your soul before He becomes visible to the world. In this way, it is the contents of your soul, not your born-again spirit directly, that the world sees.

> *When your soul comes first, fear becomes the base emotion that says, " you 're not enough."*

Your soul will inadvertently rule when the False Self or Ego is in charge, and self-centeredness becomes a byproduct. It's always clutching and fighting to "get" with regard for only itself, out of fear that it may not be

---

[11] Both Watchman Nee, *The Spiritual Man,* and Thomas Keating, *Open Mind, Open Heart,* speak of how the soul and Ego work in tandem to affect the spirit within us.

provided for if it doesn't rise up and defend its own. When your soul comes first, fear becomes the base emotion that says, "you're not enough" or "you can't measure up" to some standard you have set. This creates an ongoing sense of failing, which can result in a continuous form of striving and even wears down your physical body.

At the same time this position keeps your heart in a self-protective position not being open to the healing love of others and the Lord. Living out of this (soul) place primarily leaves us desperate for anything that will fill an empty hole. And we become emotionally, mentally, spiritually and physically vulnerable to addiction, position, achievement or love from all the wrong sources. First Peter 1:22 says, "Since you have purified your souls in obeying the truth through the Spirit in sincere love of the brethren, love one another fervently with a pure heart." Our spirit is born-again when we accept Christ, but our soul undergoes gradual transformation and sanctification as we learn to let our spirit lead. It is critical that you are freed of emotional hurts, negative thought patterns and false beliefs, so that you can live with your spirit in the lead, not your soul. This is the basis of truth from John 3:30 that says, "Less of me, more of you, Lord." Our soul was created by God not to function independently, but to submit to the Spirit's leading. It is designed to know the truth of God's love for us (as held in our spirit) and to pass that love along to others.

BODY

Your *body* is composed of your bones, flesh and blood. With your body you breathe air, eat food and live on earth. It is the visible, physical structure that houses your spirit and soul, and gives them a resting place. Your body is the temple of the Holy Spirit (1 Cor. 6:19). According to God's design, the body always follows where the soul leads—whether the soul is submitted to our spirit or it's walking independently away from God.

Hurtful emotions and false beliefs that the soul holds on to may reveal itself in the body as anxiety, depression, unhealthy behavior (sin) or physical sickness. But when the Spirit rules, the truth is present and abundant in us and shows up in your body as good health. Good health manifests into joy, peace, freedom and wholeness within you and in your relationship with God and others. Your soul can then experience health and wellness in your body.

> *Hurtful emotions and false beliefs that the soul holds on to may reveal itself in the body as anxiety or depression.*

ORDER MATTERS

These three components—spirit, soul and body—all hinge on each other. In Watchman Nee's book, *The Spiritual Man* drives home this point with this observation:

> The soul is the meeting point of spirit and body, for there they are merged. By his spirit man holds intercourse with the spiritual world and with the spirit of God, both receiving and expressing the power and life of the spiritual realm. Through his body man is in contact with the outside sensuous world, affecting it and being affected by it. The soul stands between these two worlds, yet belongs

to both. It is linked with the spiritual world through the spirit and with the material world through the body. It also possesses the power of free will, hence is able to choose from among its environments. The spirit cannot act directly upon the body. It needs a medium, and that medium is the soul produced by the touching of the spirit with the body. The soul therefore stands between the spirit and the body, binding these two together. The spirit can subdue the body through the medium of the soul, so that it will obey God; likewise the body through the soul can draw the spirit into loving the world.[12]

The order of which component comes first for you makes a difference. If your spirit leads over your soul, you are governed by "the mind of the Lord" (1 Cor. 2:16). But when the soul takes charge, you live governed by your Ego. Your False Self is actively opposed and hostile towards your spirit: "So if left to myself, the flesh is aligned with the law of sin, but now my renewed mind is fixed on and submitted to God's righteous principles" (Rom. 7:25b TPT). That's why it is so important to recognize when your flesh emerges to influence your decisions or thought life; it will directly influence whether you live from your True Self with your spirit leading, or your False Self with body or soul in the driver's seat. This is where the conflict of the old and new person begins. Because of the cross, the False Self has been crucified and is dead.

> *It is so important to recognize when your flesh emerges to influence your decisions or thought life.*

---

12 Ibid., 26.

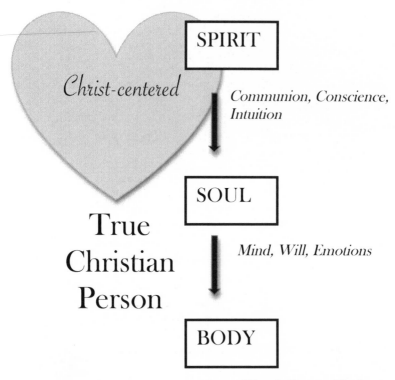

But this still leaves us with the old habits of thinking, feeling and imagining based on the programming of your past. We all have this—no matter how healthy or godly your family history was, or if you came out of a totally dysfunctional and broken background. These are old mind patterns or ways of believing that continue wanting to rule and dominate how we live and think, not realizing they have been crucified.

---

[13] Cleansing Stream Ministries taken from Cleansing Stream Workbook 2003.

Improper Spiritual Alignment[14]

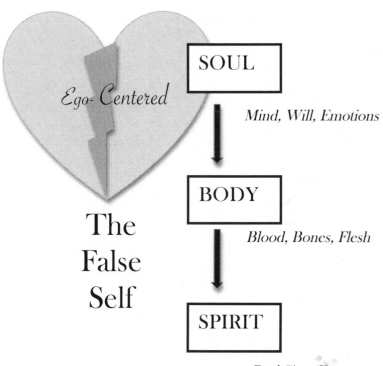

Unlike the True Self, which is based from God's love, the Ego is fear-based. Elisabeth Kübler-Ross, a pioneer and author on the stages of grief, argued there are only two emotions—love and fear—out of which all others stem from:

> It's true that there are only two primary emotions, love and fear. But it's more accurate to say that there is only love or fear, for we

[14] Ibid., Cleansing Stream Workbook 2003.

cannot feel these two emotions together, at exactly the same time. They're opposites. If we're in fear, we are not in a place of love. When we're in a place of love, we cannot be in a place of fear.[15]

> *Fear, not hate, is the opposite of love.*

We become subject to torment when we operate out of FEAR— or *False Evidence Appearing Real.*[16] Fear is the basis of all and every evil, as Satan's kingdom is aimed to mobilize torment in our hearts and minds.

Fear, not hate, is the opposite of love. That is why Scripture tells us, "There is no fear in love; but perfect love casts out fear, because fear involves torment" (1 John 4:18). It also says, "For God has not given us a spirit of fear, but of power and of love and of a sound mind" (2 Tim. 1:7). In God's kingdom, love compels us, *not fear.* Love is the foundational stone; abiding in love gives us a sound mind. But only by knowing and meditating on the love of God, can our minds function in a healthy place free from fear.

Love frees you to trust the Lord's provision and peace, but your Ego surfaces when it perceives a threat, and will try to protect itself. Anger is one of the most commons ways the Ego works to protect you. It may find other ways to mask emotional pain (self-medicating with the use of drugs and alcohol, pornography or food

---

[15] Elisabeth Kübler-Ross and David Kessler, *Life Lessons: Two Experts on Death & Dying Teach Us Abuot the Mysteries of Life & Living,* (New York: Scribner, 2000), 118-119.

[16] Ibid, 111.

for example) or by keeping itself unaware through distractions (such as work, entertainment or a hectic social life).

> *The Ego tries to impress others in making up for its perceived lack.*

I find a lot of my clients who are married or in other relationships generally struggle by reacting in anger when they have been hurt by a spouse, a family member or a friend. Often times, meanness or frustration is their default reaction, sometimes so much so, that they aren't even in touch with the pain or fear that lies beneath the rage.

You can also operate out of your Ego if you do not realize you have already been loved and accepted just as you are (Rom. 15:7). The Ego tries to impress others in making up for its perceived lack and may try to hide and pretend to be something it is not, or it may compare itself with others in such a way that looks like it comes out on top. Do you know anybody who compensates their personality with an obnoxious laugh, or flaunting all their successes in front of others? Or maybe they're always too busy for relationships with people because they place higher value on acts of service above everything else. This is a great way to determine when the Ego pops out to say, 'hello!'

The Ego can put on airs to appear very proper and moral, especially when it cloaks itself in religion, as people sometimes use "Christian-ese" language to hide behind any authenticity. When people do this, the Ego is camouflaged to mislead many. It is so easy as humans to manage our lives from the position of striving, or self-effort and working hard for the sake of our pride—so that we feel good or better about our self.

But these are hidden behind a façade of doing "good," and we often fail to recognize the Ego's work.

While attending a bible study years ago, I met a woman that was always, and I mean *always*, in a crisis. This was her definition of the ongoing problems in her life. No matter where we ran into each other, she talked of nothing else. Finally, one day I asked her if she would tell me how she was doing in all of these crises. She fumbled with her words and couldn't really express her true feelings. These crises had become her identity to such a degree that she lost who she really was as a woman of God.

> *So many of us walk around not realizing what thoughts are swirling around in our mind.*

In reference to the False Self, your Ego will only be broken by the discipline of self-denial, which is the entrance into true fellowship with Christ; "For when you live controlled by the flesh, you are about to die. But if the life of the Spirit puts to death the correct ways of the flesh, we then taste his abundant life" (Rom. 8:13 TPT).

The Ego's disguise does not fool Jesus. He warned the religious leaders of His day, first cleanse the inside of the cup and dish (a parallel referring directly to their hearts and minds), that the outside of them may also be clean: "Woe to you scribes and Pharisees, hypocrites! For you are like whitewashed tombs which indeed appear beautiful outwardly, but inside are full of dead men's bones and all uncleanness" (Matt. 23:26-27). Jesus wants us clean and right from the inside out. He wants us to walk in the completion of His work on the cross.

So many of us walk around not realizing what thoughts are swirling around in our mind. I call this walking through life unconscious. Walking with a God-consciousness is walking in self-awareness.

You will understand more of His love for you, and that surrendering the False Self with all its painful ways of fear, condemnation and bondage will help you die to your self (Matt. 16:24). Remember, you are only dying to what is ego-controlled, *not* our True Christian Person. Galatians 2:20 (MSG) says, "Indeed, I have been crucified with Christ. My Ego is no longer central."

> One's self-sufficiency is many times a Christian's prevailing sin.

God gave us free will (Gen. 2:16). Thus the soul—the seat of the mind, will and emotions—can choose to follow the leading of the Spirit or it can choose to operate out of its own independent self-sufficiency. One's self-sufficiency is many times a Christian's prevailing sin. It was even Adam and Eve's first sin in the garden when they decided the forbidden fruit was what they needed apart from God in Genesis.

If you have stepped into your Ego, don't worry—you can still recover from it and get back into your True Self. God's will for us is not for us to entertain a segmented, fractured or disconnected portion of ourselves to do the right thing. His will for you is that *all* parts and portions of you, including your past, your emotional hurts, your wrong ways of thinking or hang-ups, align with His love, His joy, His peace and His righteousness. His will for you is centered in His love and contains everything needed for healing and wholeness—for us to be our True Self.

43

God's deepest desire is that you become aware of whom you really are and allow your True Christian Person to come alive in freedom. He does not desire your True Self to be hidden behind the hurts, lies and disguises of the False Self. He wants our light—which is His light in us—to shine.

Chapter 5

ONE FOR THE TOOLKIT: SELF-LOVE

"If your compassion does not include yourself, it is incomplete."
– Jack Kornfield

In my 25 years of counseling, I have realized there are just a few basic principles at the root of most people's problems. Next to not knowing our true identity in Christ, I have found the lack of self-love—the ability to accept our self as we are and love *all* the parts of our self—is one of the basic issues that need to be addressed and brought into the light for the Lord to heal. Self-love relates to how we started with love as the key in chapter one, but self-love as a tool is practically applied through self-compassion, self-kindness, encouragement and surrender. This became clear to me as I began teaching my clients and participants in my classes about their true identity. It appeared most of them had a hard time even being able to picture their own value, much less being able to love themselves.

> *Loving yourself is not the same as the narcissistic self-centeredness of entitlement.*

The result of you learning and applying self-love creates such a phenomenal new way of thinking with the mind of Christ (1 Cor. 2:16). Loving yourself is not the same as the narcissistic self-centeredness of entitlement. It's not about the generation or culture that believes, "It's all about me." It embodies the practice of grace before truth, surrounded by love instead of judgment.[17]

In all my studies and research, and next to the Holy Spirit's voice, I have found self-love to be the best tool for accomplishing a correct perspective and value on who you truly are, and how to see and value yourself *as He sees you* (Rom. 7:17, TPT).

These four components of self-love—compassion, kindness, encouragement and surrender—will empower you how to love *all* of you, so when you find yourself offended by someone, fall short of perfection, or fail in any way, you can still stand (Eph. 6:13). Incorporating these tools into your daily time with God will empower you to live

> *Self-compassion teaches us to accept emotions as neither good nor bad——it acknowledges them as emotions in and of themselves.*

[17] This principle is my own version of one of Graham Cooke's "8 Relationship Guidelines" developed from a working group at the Mission Church in Vacaville, Calif.

free to love and forgive yourself and others in their deficiencies. I've found great success (for both me and my clients) to minister self-love throughout the day. If you don't, you will find yourself much more vulnerable to all sorts of hurts, offenses, pent-up anger, hate and other unwanted feelings that rob you from living your true life in God.

SHOW YOURSELF COMPASSION

Self-compassion is sometimes confused with empathy. Although similar, empathy is being able to relate to someone else's emotions, which can sometimes lead to being caught up in those emotions ourselves. If a person has just lost a loved one in death, then this could naturally trigger your own pain if you have also experienced the loss of a loved one.

Compassion allows having a heart connection on a deeper emotional level than just empathy alone, and also has the emotional maturity to stay grounded in the True Christian Person without allowing someone else's life and emotions to drive or trigger your own.

Self-compassion teaches us to accept emotions as neither good nor bad—it acknowledges them as emotions in and of themselves. When you do your self-compassion, it is okay to feel pain, whether you felt you deserved it or not. But it is not permitting or excusing sin or mistakes, and it does not judge your actions or your offender's. Self-compassion does not say, "It's okay; what they did to you was wrong"—but, "I understand how you feel; we'll do better next time."

As you begin using this newfound tool, it is important to not only change your self-talk to become more loving and compassionate, but also picture yourself through

47

the eyes of the person that Jesus sees. The purpose for picturing yourself through your sanctified imagination is because your subconscious mind thinks mostly in pictures through your visual sense. Your subconscious is the ultimate decision maker. As you picture your True Self along with Jesus being in control, you are creating positive change to happen in your current, real-life situation automatically. You will be living out of this loving, compassionate self that is strong in the Lord without even working at it.

> Once you learn to step out of your own pain and become the observer, you have taken authority over your wounded self.

Here's a great way you can apply self-compassion:

Start by picturing in your mind's eye Jesus and the True Christian Person in your secret place. Then, securely fastened in your True Christian Person, look out of your True Self's eyes with Jesus right by your side.

Now picture the 'you' who's just been rejected or hurt standing in front of you both. This is the False (human) Self, your Ego, or your flesh who's become wounded and concluded it's not being wanted, or being disrespected—you name the pain or offense.

With Jesus next to you, go to the wounded self and say, "(your name), I love you." Now show compassion in the situation or circumstance, saying you understand and would feel the same way. Allow Jesus to speak a compassionate word and tell (the False Self) how much

He loves them. Showing love in this way brings such honor and validation to our wounded part.

Separating your True Self from the deeply wounded part, or False Self, is the basic key—and being able to see the two separately is very important. This insures you stay out of your own wounding and pain (so you don't relive the experience).

You have to do this daily and multiple times a day, especially if you become offended or hurt. As you allow Jesus to love you consistently like this, you will remain filled for whenever you are in need of the love that people cannot extend to you. The Bible encourages us this way: "Put on truth as a belt to strengthen you to stand in triumph. Put on holiness as the protective armor that covers your heart" (Eph. 6:14 TPT).

Once you learn to step out of your own pain and become the observer, you have taken authority over your wounded self, or the Ego that's trying to defend or protect itself. You are no longer held captive by your emotions and you are free from a victim mentality you felt as that wounded person.

At first, you might only be able to step out of your pain for a short period of time; but don't worry because this is a process. You will continue to grow in strength as the True Self becomes stronger and the wounded emotions become healed.

With consistent practice, you will soon be able to walk in complete freedom without the power of the pain overtaking you.

BE KIND TO YOURSELF

One of the fruit's of the Spirit stated in scripture is kindness (Gal. 5:22). Proverbs 19:22 says, "What is desired in a man is kindness."

Kindness is closely related to compassion, but being kind to yourself includes setting boundaries that help take care of you. Having good, healthy boundaries protects your mental, physical, emotional and spiritual boundary limits to help you distinguish what is and is not your responsibility.[18] Being kind to yourself can include anything from taking a hot bath, having quiet time, exercising and eating right (even a little bit of chocolate), and getting plenty of sleep. It's taking time to take care of you so you can be healthy for the mission and purpose to which God has called you.

> *If you don't recognize your own inward need of kindness toward yourself, you will see yourself either as undeserving or totally dismiss the need.*

If you don't recognize your own inward need of kindness toward yourself, you will see yourself either as undeserving or totally dismiss the need. Maybe you feel you aren't being humble or are afraid you'll think too highly of yourself and become arrogant. Or maybe you are concerned about being selfish if you do show yourself kindness.

If you live by the twisted version of the Golden Rule— that if you are kind to others, they will automatically be

---

[18] Henry Cloud and John Townsend, *Boundaries: When to Say Yes, How to Say No to Take Control of Your Life.* (Grand Rapids: Zondervan, 1992), 27.

kind back—then this will result in expecting others to fill your need for kindness. The problem with this mindset is when others fail us—*which, they will*—you will find yourself offended because your expectation was for others to be kind to you, before you placed value and were kind to yourself.

ENCOURAGE YOURSELF

Encouragement gives us hope. Romans 5:5 tells us, "Now hope does not disappoint because the love of God has been poured out in our hearts by the Holy Spirit who was given to us." Encouragement nurtures patience and kindness, and helps us persevere through times of trials and hardship.

Encouraging yourself makes it easier to love and live in this world with all of its struggles and pain. Without encouragement, life would feel pointless and burdensome, and it would be easy to feel overwhelmed and unloved.

> *Encouragement nurtures patience and kindness, and it helps us persevere through times of trials and hardship.*

If you never experience any encouraging words beckoning you forward—"Come on, you've got this; you're doing great, keep going!"—life can become too tedious and thankless to even want to keep pressing through those dark times we all experience. Encouragement validates the gifts and talents placed within you, and consoles the person who faces a tough situation or circumstance. Next to Jesus, you need to be your own best champion.

You need to know how to declare victory for yourself and then also believe and have faith that you have it, because scripture says you do. You are victorious in Him: "In this world you will have trouble. But take heart! I have overcome the world" (John 16:33 NIV).

One man I know faces a lot of discouragement at work with his boss and peers with many verbal put-downs and being ousted from social circles. He goes in day after day underutilized and unchallenged in his job. His boss undermines much of his decisions in front on his team, and there is little incentive to work hard. Can he walk through this undefeated, encouraging himself, and keeping his joy in tact?

> *You and the Holy Spirit should be your biggest fan base.*

The man needs to picture his True Christian Person with Jesus, and firstly, go alongside that hurting man that's being assaulted with all the verbal and social rejection to show compassion and acknowledge the pain he's experiencing at work. In his mind's eye, his adult Christian man and Jesus also need to work hand-in-hand to encourage him along—that he *is* doing a good job; that he *is* faithful in his job despite how he's treated at work; that his work report and reputation are ultimately trusted in the hands of God *and not his boss.* Only then can the Lord show him the truth regarding his own feelings and bring healing to his heart by assuring him that God will work it all out for his good (Rom. 8:28).

It is time you start believing in your heart what His word says about you. You are a victor not a victim of your own life. You and the Holy Spirit should be your biggest fan base. So often we go against and resist what the Lord is saying to us when He is really cheering us on. It is time you partner with Him and encourage and believe you are everything He says you are. Remember *encouragement produces hope*, and ultimately helps us experience the abundant life that Jesus promises us (John 10:10).

SURRENDERING IT ALL

As I talk with people regarding the need to surrender to the Lord, I find their definition of surrender is "giving up." This is especially a common understanding with those who I have talked and counseled who have served in the military. In the U.S. Armed Services Code of Conduct, military members are actually taught this principle: "I will never surrender of my own free will. If in command, I will never surrender the members of my command while they still have the means to resist."[19] The only problem with this definition and visual reference is that it goes directly against what the Bible teaches us about God's promises. There is a big difference between surrendering to the enemy and surrendering to God. Surrendering to the enemy means defeat; surrendering to the Lord means victory!

> *There is a big difference between surrendering to the enemy and surrendering to God.*

When you surrender to Jesus, it isn't about "giving up" and quitting as with an enemy, but *"giving over"* your

---

[19] Article II taken from the Code of Conduct for the United States Armed Forces.

will and your plans in loving trust to God. This requires letting go of your need to control the situation or the issue at hand. Sometimes the fear of the unknown and the thought of flailing out of control are so great, you could actually lose out on the very thing you want and what He wants for you *if you don't let go, or surrender.* Once you begin understanding His love for you, surrendering to His will becomes so much easier. God has and always will have the best in mind for you and your future (Jer. 29:11). Surrendering your plan over to God is centered in His plans for you becoming the very best that you can be. Remember, you are the only one the Lord has designed to fulfill your life's purpose and plan.

Matthew 11:28-30 says, "Come to Me, all you who labor and are heavy laden, and I will give you rest. Take My yoke upon you and *learn from Me,* for I am gentle and lowly in heart, and you will find rest for your souls. For My yoke is easy and My burden is light." If you want to reap the rewards from true surrender, then you must be willing to *learn from Him.* This takes trusting and believing in the Lord's goodness, allowing Jesus to teach you His ways. Surrendering all of your burdens or worries you carry to Him helps you to continually grow stronger in your faith and give up the belief that somehow it's up to you to work off your burdens.

This concept is so difficult for those of us who have strived for so long. God understands self-sufficiency was humanity's original sin against him (Gen. 3:6-7) and a great struggle for us, so He wants to teach us about surrender. This is why doing it daily is so important; the promise is "God's wonderful peace that transcends human understanding" and entering into His rest (Phil. 4:7 TPT). Nothing is more restful than a life filled with love, peace and joy with Him completely free from all striving. The component of surrender will directly affect your freedom from the anxieties life brings your way. Worry, stress, and anxiety are all fear-based emotions that throw us into the False Self. Scripture tells us, "be anxious for nothing, but in everything by prayer and supplication, with thanksgiving, let your requests be made known to God" (Phil. 4:6). Supplication is the attitude or spirit of surrendering your requests in prayer. It is making yourself humble before God as you submit your will to His will, and to His authority. As you pray with thanksgiving and gratitude to Jesus, you will find your emotion of fear is replaced with love and faith in God's promises for you. You will find yourself filled with a new joy, excited and empowered to surrender because of the anticipation of what God has waiting for you.

THE HIGH STAKES OF SELF-LOVE

Self-love is the ability to recognize and accept the flaws in yourself, as well as the beautiful attributes you carry.

> *Self-love is the ability to recognize and accept the flaws in yourself, as well as the beautiful attributes you carry.*

We all have faults, but the secret is to have complete, total self-acceptance that you are God's work in progress. It also is tremendously easy to dismiss loving ourselves (and not administer self-love) because we can so easily feel we don't deserve love. This is very common, especially if you grew up in a family who disregarded you, abused you, or withheld hugs, or any kind of love from you when you needed it. This can even rise up if rude people cut you off in traffic, or cut in front of you in the line at the store. If someone really loved us, why would they have treated us that way?

What often happens when the Lord communicates how much He loves you, your Ego can immediately step in as an inner critic and argue God's truth about you; it can sound or feel personally degrading, or somehow cover up the truth with a destructive lie. This can be hard to detect sometimes because we hear it in first person:

> *The Ego will use every trick it can, anytime it can, to try and convince you that you need to improve yourself to deserve God's love.*

"How could anyone love me like this?"

"That was the most stupid thing I could have done."

"I've blown it...again."

The Ego will use every trick it can, anytime it can, to try and convince you that you need to improve yourself to deserve your heavenly Father's love. We dismiss, minimize, and devalue our feelings because we don't feel or believe we have a right to them. This can creep up in many forms from your past, or could just be outright malice you might encounter from other people on a daily basis.

Too often we believe that if we aren't suffering at a major extent, we don't have the right to show ourselves empathy. This is not God's truth (Ps. 56:8 NLT). The Lord cares about every hair on your head, so of course, He cares if you are hurt or upset. These are the times to give yourself love with compassion and encouragement.

I have found some of the most common ways the enemy can deceive people is through the False Self; it can manifest criticism, negative self-talk or self-condemning judgment as a response, or just flat out lie to you about what you have to do to earn His love. Jesus' word, which is living and powerful, is the only thing that will cut through it all (Rom. 7:25).

Growing up, the rule in my home was: if Mom was cleaning, all of the kids better be cleaning also. No sitting around watching TV while others are working. We didn't want to be labeled as "lazy"; we also needed to have all our chores done before we got to play. These rules instilled wonderful work ethics in us as kids, but it took me a long time as an adult to realize I could spend my time first thing in the morning in prayer (because I felt it was a luxury) instead of cleaning the house. (I still have to make my bed first.)

I believe it is very easy for us to take on the role of the critical parent in our mind if we allow fear to rule us. Fear can convince us that if we are not critical and judgmental to ourselves, we won't get things done. You could even fear becoming lazy or slothful, especially if you were raised with a highly critical or demanding parent. If your parents had a high work ethic but not much balance with compassion, I can almost bet you will find yourself being very strict, unkind and demanding of yourself, your work, and those around you.

> *If you are prone or susceptible to perfectionism, it is very difficult for you to not have a critical spirit.*

This judgmental inner critic cancels out the soft gentle voice of the Holy Spirit. Once you have practiced this self-love tool, you can silence the inner critic's words and transition into experiencing a beautiful and amazing peace free from criticism and shame. The Holy Spirit's loving words will begin to overrule the lies of the inner critic with His Power. This leaves room for your True Self and the Holy Spirit to be in one accord—and it will accelerate the overall healing of your old negative thinking.

With self-compassion we understand that encouragement—*not* criticism—is the lever that motivates us to persevere, press in and keep going. Kristin Neff, a Ph.D. widely recognized as one of the world's leading experts on self-compassion, talks about self-kindness and why it's important:

> We stop the constant self-judgment and disparaging internal commentary that most of us have come to see as normal. It requires us to understand our foibles and failures instead of condemning them. It entails seeing the extent to which we harm ourselves through relentless self-criticism, and ending our internal war.[20]

One way I was not showing self-love was when others would reject my ideas, or not accept my teachings that I knew in my heart the Lord had given me. I would recoil in self-doubt and lose confidence and my trust in the Lord, and I started to worry that I was on the wrong path and I had heard Him wrong. I would continually go back to my prayer closet and hope to hear from Him again and again, reassuring me that I was on the right path. This went on for a long time, until God

---

[20] Kristin Neff, *Self-Compassion: the Proven Power of Being Kind to Yourself,* (New York: HarerCollins Publishers, 2011), 42.

finally showed me that I was not only *not* trusting Him, but also not trusting or believing in the passion and truths He had poured into me initially.

I had to start showing myself love, compassion and encouragement on a daily basis—and several times throughout the day to quiet the negative self-talk of "straighten up and fly right...or you're a failure and a loser." I had to realize and know in my heart of hearts that God had already extended His love, encouragement, gifts and talents to me, and I needed to do likewise. Otherwise, I was continually self-sabotaging my growth in becoming all He intended.

It only took a few months to renew my heart and mind until I felt strong in Him and no longer believed I needed man's opinion or approval to help me go forward. This was something I had battled with for years. It was quite an experience to finally be able to live with only needing God's word that said, "*YES!*" and was solid in my heart. I was ecstatic with this newfound freedom.

SELF LOVE IN THE DAILY GRIND: HOW THIS ALL FITS TOGETHER

Now that you understand all the aspects of self-love and how it renews, heals, and silences the inner critic, it is necessary to apply and practice this discipline throughout your daily life. You will need to listen to your own inner thoughts and instantly replace the negative ones with your new self-love tool several times a day. This is what renews your mind and builds your new mind circuitry, so you now can establish the mind of Christ deep within you.[21]

This will also keep you out of any judgment of others. Maybe you have taken control over your tongue (and the words that come out of your mouth) but are still having critical thoughts; rest assured, dropping down into picturing your True Christian Person and ministering self-love in those moments will help change your own negative self-talk to be more loving and compassionate. If you are prone or susceptible to perfectionism, it is very difficult for you to *not* have a critical spirit. If this is the case with you, I have listed below a couple of questions to ask yourself:

❑ Are your default thoughts and inner commentary more of a critical nature than they are positive and complimentary toward yourself and others?

❑ When you are observing something, are your thoughts or comments critical before they are positive or complimentary?

❑ These questions will give you a pretty good indication of how critical you are being with yourself.

Learning to be mindful and totally aware of your inner thoughts is a discipline that is powerfully strengthened while meditating on His word. You cannot bring renewal to your thought life if you aren't aware of what your thoughts are saying. This is a prerequisite in order to silence the inner critic from all of the destructive, negative words that ruminate through your mind.

---

[21] Daniel J. Siegel, *Mindsight: The New Science of Personal Transformation,* (New York: Batnam Books, 2011), 84-86.

A new set of words that comfort and encourage need to be formed to replace those old negative ones: "He comforts and encourages us in our suffering so we may comfort and encourage others in theirs" (2 Cor. 1:4 AMP). You'll even be filled with a new level of love for others. The people who were impossible to love will become miraculously easier for you to love and live among as an automatic result of the fruit of love.

THE POWER OF SELF-LOVE APPLIED

A client I worked closely with in the past was a very kind, gracious and loving woman—but she was a total doormat. Her negative self-talk was nothing short of abusive. She had accepted her mom's abusive words as her own that were spoken to her constantly from early childhood and carried them in her mind into early adult years. These words kept her feeling beaten down throughout most of her life—and it not only crippled her relationship with her mother, but also with her husband who had somewhat of the same tendencies (although not as violent).

> *You cannot bring renewal to your thought life if you aren't aware of what your thoughts are saying.*

The result of such verbal abuse left her living in constant fear and anxiety and she suffered with severe depression and acute anxiety disorder, which she had been diagnosed as having. She told me she wanted to be rid of these fears and anxieties once and for all, and after seeing many counselors and psychiatrists with very little results, she was ready to try my faith-based counseling.

Due to the abusive family dialogue she endured growing up, which was also a generational hand-me-down, she continued hearing and replaying in her mind the same old critical, fearful thoughts.

She projected the intensity of these feelings onto others. Consequently, she could never stand up to any angry person or know how to handle any conflict or difficult situation. This left her living in constant fear and anxiety with not only family members, but with anyone who had an assertive or aggressive personality.

She started practicing being kind to herself by establishing good boundaries—first with others, then with herself. These boundaries included going back to the gym for her physical well-being; for her emotional well being, she stopped all ruminating thoughts (recycling over and over) on any negative thinking. Her discipline of taking every thought captive eventually led to her freedom from the negative thoughts from entering into her mind at all. She was amazed at how quickly she learned how to be kind to herself.

By changing her negative self-talk to words of compassion, she was able to block the inner critic, and this helped her hear the Lord speak His loving words to her. She knew the words in her mind from what the Bible said were true, but she wasn't ever able to believe them down in her heart. Her growth in living out of her True Self was rapid and beautiful.

Then she started being able to confront others regarding her own feelings by continually encouraging herself regarding her own worth. Because of her naturally gracious and loving personality, she was able to confront others in perfect love and gentleness. She learned how to live as the powerful woman of God by surrendering her fears over to the Lord. After many years in a very difficult marriage, she now lives with the same man in a total victorious life filled with love, respect and being honored as the beautiful woman of God that she is.

Neff says, "Self-kindness involves more than merely stopping self-judgment. It involves actively comforting ourselves, responding just as we would to a dear friend in need. It means we allow ourselves to be emotionally moved by our own pain."[22]

Just like with my frightened client, you have to take back your God-given authority over your mind and shut down that fearful inner critic. It wants to rule over your entire life and cause you so much unnecessary pain. *Remember, it is God's word and love that is supposed to rule and reign over your mind, will, and emotions.*

When you love yourself and embrace your own human flaws, you are empowered to live authentically and vulnerably in the freedom Jesus purchased for you; it gives you permission to fail and still know how much you are loved.

---

[22] Kristin Neff, *Self-Compassion*, 42.

Chapter 6

LISTENING TO LOVE OTHERS

"Most people do not listen with the intent to understand. They listen with the intent to reply" – Stephen R. Covey

Having gained a whole new understanding of how to be more compassionate with yourself, you have not only learned to experience love from Jesus in a much deeper way, but you've acquired the new ability to now pass this love on to others. As the Lord showed me how to practically love myself with all the tools of self-compassion, my love for people was upgraded to a more unconditional acceptance despite people's rage or anger that came out of their Ego.

I started listening without judgment and had a new level of compassion toward them, especially as they shared and opened up with me about how abusive they had been to others. This is the benefit of how self-love pays huge rewards. The number one way you continue to pay self-love forward is by how well you can listen to others.

Listening with true love for people became a natural part of me and how I lived. How effectively you listen to someone will immediately determine how well he or she feels loved, respected, and valued as a fellow human being, and this is what builds strong relationships. I'm not just talking about only hearing their spoken words; I mean taking the time to really listen to understand them. This specifically demands two things of you: validating others' emotions and feelings, and expressing authentic empathy with compassion in their situation.

> *How effectively you listen to someone will immediately determine how well someone feels loved, respected or valued.*

Because of learning and applying self-love (as you did in the chapter before), God has strengthened your True Christian Person (inner man or woman) in a very powerful way—and you will now be prepared to listen to others without having your negative inner critic judging or critiquing them. Consequently, your relationships will take on much deeper meaning. These practical ways and techniques will really help unlock your ability to pass love onto others and make you a successful, loving listener.

BEING A LOVING LISTENER

After many years of counseling, teaching, and training groups in the subject of effective listening, I have found the lack of being a good listener a major factor in most troubled relationships. James 1:19 (NLT) states, "Understand this, my dear brothers and sisters: You must all be quick to listen, slow to speak and slow to get angry."

Without having a loving listener to talk with, it's easy to end up feeling lonely and shut out. The art of listening is like giving a beautiful gift of love and acceptance to the other person because it confirms their value and importance as a human being.

If a young mom is home all day raising young children while her husband is climbing the corporate ladder, she might find her words and trials of the day fall on deaf ears when he arrives home. This could be a result of the husband's own self-absorption regarding the stress from his job, or being too tired to deal with anything else emotionally. These circumstances can easily leave the wife feeling lonely and closed off from his world unless they know how to take the special time each day to listen to one another.

Being a loving listener is a gift because it requires setting your own agenda aside for another. If done correctly, you will be placing the feelings, thoughts and emotions that another person is dealing with, over your own. Knowing how to listen, with the ability and discipline to hear the person's heart, or intent, is of vital importance in every relationship. It is a basic need of all of us to be known for who we really are (1 Cor. 13:12 NLT).

In order to truly listen with your whole heart, being present, trustworthy and unconditionally loving others are requirements that build relationships so you can validate their emotions and feelings, and show empathy and compassion at a deeper level.

Being present means being fully mindful and attentive in the moment you are experiencing, not falling into the past or jumping into the future. This gives the person who is speaking with you the gift of feeling known and being loved. This includes giving them your undivided attention and having the true desire to really understand with empathy what is being said—this is listening so you can hear what is sacred and meaningful at the core of who they are.

Another factor of being a good, loving listener is being a trustworthy one. Since the foundation of every good relationship is based on trust, it is very important that you are a safe recipient with those whom you are communicating.[23] Being trustworthy safeguards another's vulnerability, too. A person sharing their feelings becomes very vulnerable because they're taking a risk opening their heart and trusting you will protect it. Allowing others to feel and express their emotional pain without you passing judgment protects their openness with you.

So for example—if I choose to engage in a conversation with you over something that offended you, I am choosing (and risking) to hear how upset you may be with me. I have to open up my heart and be vulnerable with you, as you have to with me. In doing so, I risk hearing things that may hurt my feelings or listen to things you may say that I may totally disagree with. This is a huge emotional risk I take with you, as well as

---

[23] Henry Cloud and John Townsend, *Safe People: How to find relationships that are good for you and avoid those that aren't,* (Grand Rapids: Zondervan, 1995), 35.

you with me. Despite someone's emotional maturity, emotional risk is something we need to embrace in order to form intimate relationships. If done with the love and grace of God, then the payoff is well worth the cost.

Unconditional love requires us to be free of any criticism or judgment toward others, which is directly related to how we look at and judge ourselves. Self-judgment will derail you from being able to truly listen, because being critical of yourself leaves you at risk to be critical of others.

A critical spirit, which stems from not loving all parts of yourself, will cloud or distort your ability to hear them accurately, especially if there is a sin you've committed of which you don't feel you deserve forgiveness. Practicing self-love minimizes your own self-judgment, and can shut criticism down completely. Then, you can unconditionally love others without the fear of being critical or judgmental toward them; this gives you the freedom to easily love others without the expectation or need of being loved by them in return. Unconditionally loving others is now possible.

> *A critical spirit, which stems from not loving all parts of yourself, will cloud or distort your ability to hear them accurately.*

TOOLS OF EFFECTIVE LISTENING: VALIDATION & EMPATHY

To validate someone is to first accept and acknowledge someone's present feelings as his or her own. It is not agreeing or approving of what is being said; rather, it is a way of supporting all they are dealing with in their thoughts and emotions. This strengthens the relationship and allows you both to maintain different opinions. Validation is important in listening to someone because it is the first way you can begin to show someone acceptance.

Here are some really simple ways to validate someone in a conversation:

- Yeah / Mmmm / Awww
- I hear you.
- That hurts.
- That's not good.
- That's no fun.
- Wow, that's a lot to deal with.
- I would feel the same way (of that emotion) too.
- That is sad.
- That sounds discouraging.
- That sounds like it would really hurt.
- That must really hurt.
- I can understand why you'd be upset under these circumstances.
- Anyone would find this difficult.
- Most people would feel the same way.
- Your reactions are totally normal.

To lead a conversation using validation, you can use:

- I can see that you are really upset.
- You look pretty sad.
- You seem a little worried, troubled, scared, etc.
- Would you like to talk about it?
- That really bothered you, didn't it?
- How did you feel when (the event) happened?

You can validate others in conversation with these simple questions:

- ◆ Really?
- ◆ Yeah?
- ◆ How so?

- ◆ You did?
- ◆ How come?
- ◆ How's that?

- ◆ She did?
- ◆ How's that?

Remember, validation is acknowledging a person has something to say. Validating the other person's emotions immediately reveals your respect for them. This does not mean they have to earn your respect in order for you to give respect. It is conveying recognition of the feelings they are experiencing. Validation is powerful in helping you begin the journey to build trust and empower someone to continue sharing.

EMPATHY WITH COMPASSION

I use empathy and compassion interchangeably, because they basically use the same response. Empathy with compassion works together to relieve suffering or relate with people in their pain or joy. Cindy Wigglesworth, the author of SQ21: The Twenty One Skills of Spiritual Intelligence talks about how empathy engages an attitude that is committed to being fully understanding, while "Compassion goes a step further—while you feel what the other feels, you don't get lost in the feelings. Informed by wisdom, you have a loving desire to alleviate the suffering of others."[24]

There is no fear, panic or anxiety in compassion because it partners with wisdom to see God's larger

---

[24] Cindy Wigglesworth, SQ21: The Twenty One Skills of Spiritual Intelligence, (New York: SelectBooks, Inc., 2012), 74.

picture, perspective or strategy. They are only separate by your ability to stay detached from the emotions of others, which allows you to use your God-given wisdom when you listen.

God is our original example of empathy with compassion; He can feel the depth of our pain. Although the word "empathy" doesn't appear in scripture, there are many indirect references, specifically the scriptures that mention compassion or when Jesus wept. Paul wrote, "Rejoice with those who rejoice, and weep with those who weep" (Rom. 12:15).

In the New Testament, we see Jesus use compassion in several instances right before He healed someone.

> *God is our original example of empathy with compassion.*

In the story of Jesus' friend Lazarus, Jesus shows us His true empathy for Mary: "Therefore, when Jesus saw her weeping, and the Jews that came with her weeping, He groaned in the spirit and was troubled" (John 11:33). This story goes on to show us the Lord's love and compassion: "Jesus wept. Then the Jews said, 'See how He loved him" (John 11:35, 36). These indirect references refer to the same thing: "the ability to share someone else's feelings."[25]

Let's take a look at some examples of empathetic responses:

- ◆ As I see it, you are _____.
- ◆ You appear to be feeling _____.

---

[25] "Compassion." *Merriam-Webster.com*. 2011. http://www.merriam-webster.com/dictionary/empathy.

- I'm sensing that you feel _____.
- From what I'm hearing, you feel _____.
- I get the impression you are _____.
- It is almost like you are saying _____.
- I'm hearing where you are coming from is a place of _____.
- It sounds to me like you are feeling _____.
- I imagine right now that you feel _____.
- That sounds very painful.
- I can't even imagine something that horrific.
- You must feel exhausted having to endure that for so long.
- Despite your feeling so bad, you are still coping so well.
- That is quite an accomplishment! I am very impressed by how well you are dealing with the uncertainty.

When it comes to listening effectively, empathy is the spiritual and emotional antidote for healing wounds in others, and with self-compassion, it becomes the healing balm for us. Speaking encouraging words that are filled with empathy focuses on the positive aspects of your conversation and further enhances connection with your listener.

Dr. David Sac, M.D. states that he believes empathy is a core part of what makes us human:

> Empathy is key to all human social interaction and morality [...] Without empathy, we would have no cohesive society, no trust and no reason not to murder, cheat, steal or lie. At best, we would act only out of self-interest; at worst, we would be a collection of sociopaths.[26]

---

[26] David Sac, Psych Central, "Is Empathy an Outdated Concept?" August 28, 2015. http://blogs.psychcentral.com/addiction-recovery/2012/03/empathy

A part of our brain is designed to function in empathy resulting in personal healing and restoration. In *The God Shaped Brain*, author Timothy R. Jennings, M.D. explains how God made our brain to experience empathy even if we haven't been trained in or exposed to it: "The Anterior Cingulate Cortex (ACC) is, neurologically speaking, the 'heart' of the brain. It is in the brain region where we experience empathy, compassion, and love, and where we choose the right from the wrong."[27] Jennings goes on to say, "Only love, coming from God, is capable of freeing us from fear. Brain-imaging studies have demonstrated that the more time a person spends in communion with the God of love, the more developed the ACC becomes."[28]

Even for children to grow to be compassionate and caring people, we must recognize the need of teaching and training them the importance of empathy and validation at an early age. In the same article with Jennings, Maia Szalavitz who is a neuroscience journalist and author of the book *Unbroken Brain: Why Addiction Is a Learning Disorder and Why It Matters* says, "Increasingly, neuroscientists, psychologists and educators believe that bullying and other kinds of violence can indeed be reduced by encouraging empathy at an early age."[29]

From the years I've worked as a counselor, it's exciting to see how these studies show how science and God are

---

[27] Timothy R. Jennings, *The God-Shaped Brain: How changing your view of God transforms your life,* (Downers Grove: InterVarsity Press, 2013), 38.

[28] Ibid., 42.

[29] David Sac, Psych Central, "Is Empathy an Outdated Concept?" August 28, 2015. http://blogs.psychcentral.com/addiction-recovery/2012/03/empathy

authenticating one another, which is an inspiration to press forward teaching others the power of God's word.

LISTENING TO LOVE IN ACTION

One client of mine, whose wife did not share his same level of spiritual or emotional maturity, came to me seeking help after trying other forms of counseling and marriage courses. Fear had kept his wife from seeking healing from her early years of severe abuse. My client (the husband) was desperate and didn't have much hope for the marriage lasting. He was willing to own responsibility for his part and knew he had his own Ego work to do. He also came to realize he had some old wounds that needed healing. He learned that if he could set his own Ego aside and accept his True Self in Christ, he would be in a better place to love and understand her with greater empathy and compassion.

In the beginning, he got pulled into her blaming accusations and verbal abuse because of his own desire to defend and protect himself. As he learned self-compassion and how to meditate on God's word, his responses to his wife took a 180-degree turn; he started validating her, even in the midst of her angry outbursts. He learned how to give her the empathy and compassion he never had been able to show her previously. He was now totally free to love her without putting up his walls of self-protection.

Because he practiced being such a loving listener, he became her safe person, which was something she never experienced with anyone. She could now trust her heart to him at a level she never felt before. Because of the change she saw in him, she started working on her own deep wounds. Although this isn't a completed happily every after story, my client felt so blessed and full of God's love, that in faith he believes she will receive complete healing. He is not only committed to her forever, but also to continuing his own work using the healing disciplines with the Lord.

You can grow from the negative interactions with people, but the positive attributes in others should challenge you as well. Your loved ones and friends should continually be challenging you to become the best you can be in Christ with their encouraging words, support and love. The Lord continually puts people in your path to grow you, whether it is in easy loving circumstances, or difficult, stressful ones. Opening your heart to hear what the Holy Spirit wants to tell you, either through His gentle voice or the voice of others, will help you to continue to grow in His image of humility and love.

THINGS TO AVOID WHEN LISTENING

As you increase trustworthiness between your relationships, creating an atmosphere where others can be vulnerable will help you provide a safe space for people to open up about what's on their heart and mind. In doing that, there are certain things that are important to avoid when listening to someone who is sharing a close matter with you.

> *Your Ego is more concerned about being heard, loved or respected than it is about being loving or respectful toward others.*

When you show people love by listening effectively, your Ego will war in this process with your True Christian Person as it fights to maintain its control to be heard. This is really where the Ego has the greatest risk of getting in the way because our human nature can respond quickly or defensively. Your Ego is more concerned about being heard, loved or respected than it is about being loving or respectful toward others. This blocks us from hearing what the other person has to say.

I call this JERDing: it's when you try to Justify, Explain, Rationalize or Defend yourself. This is the Ego's form of protection. When you listen to someone, you are not the focus; they are. So keep your Ego out and stay in your True Christian Person.

Do not Justify yourself; instead continue listening to hear their whole story.

> *"Remember, your side of the story will only be understood when you first understand."*
> *– St. Francis of Assisi*

Do not try to Explain yourself as to why or why not you said or did something.

Do not Rationalize your behavior or words.

Do not Defend yourself; instead listen to understand how the other person feels.

Listening includes not interrupting, not thinking about your own judgments to what's being said, and not waiting for an opportunity to speak. Even though you may not agree with everything that is being said, this isn't the time to share your thoughts or opinions.

When it is your turn to respond, there are some guidelines to help you avoid triggering any negative emotions in the other person. The goal is that you not compound any hurt they may be experiencing as you hear them open up to you.

Be careful not say, "I understand." Even though you may, or probably do, the other person has no way of knowing you understand. Instead, respond by saying how you might feel if that happened to you. Then ask if you were accurate; you will be able to tell right away if they feel understood.

Do not take a turn to share a similar situation about yourself (thinking you will convince them that you understand). This only puts the focus on you and leaves the other person hanging in a painful place. If you interrupt to interject something about you, be aware that you have brought the focus back to yourself. You may use a short quick statement that says, "Yes, I have experienced something similar," but bring it right back to the other person.

THE IMPORTANCE OF BODY LANGUAGE

Body language is a tool you can use strategically to support someone who wants to share their heart with you, but if you're not aware of what your body is doing, you can also be subconsciously sending the wrong message to the person who's talking with you.

Letting your body language convey empathy is an easy way to begin communication. Body language that shows your empathy and support when listening include:

- Keeping your body open and facing the other person.
- Nodding your head in acknowledgment (without becoming a "bobble head").
- Making eye contact with the other person.

Body language that can sabotage your communication in listening includes:

+ Fidgeting.
+ Folding or crossing your arms.
+ No eye contact, to include rolling your eyes.
+ Being distracted (on your phone, laptop, or with the current surroundings).

An open body posture that does not close off or block your body conveys that you are ready to listen to someone. Dr. Albert Mehrabian, author of Silent Messages, conducted several studies on nonverbal communication. He found that only seven percent of any message is conveyed through words. And while a person's vocal intonation affected the listener by 38 percent, 55 percent of communication came through nonverbal elements (facial expression, gestures, posture, etc.).[30] Some dispute this finding, stating the amount of communication that's nonverbal is approximately 60-90 percent (depending upon the situation and the people involved).[31] Either way, the science behind how much nonverbal communication we engage in is substantial.

THE CHALLENGES OF LISTENING

All types and cultures of people will challenge your ability to stay in a loving place on a regular (if not daily)

---

[30] BusinessBalls. Mehrabian's communication research. "Professor Albert Mehrabian's communications model" August 27, 2016. http://www.businessballs.com/mehrabiancommunications.htm.

[31] The Nonverbal Group. "How Much of Communication is Really Nonverbal?" http://www.nonverbalgroup.com/2011/08/how-much-of-communication-is-really-nonverbal.

basis by things they say or do. We're human; and in our humanness we all are susceptible to messing up or accidentally offending someone. Your responsibility as a Christ-follower is to respond from a place of love, grace, mercy and understanding to what you encounter—from anyone. In order to do so properly, you must remain centered in your True Self and not allow the influence of your Ego to override your spirit. By doing this, you will model for others the love of Jesus.

This is not an easy task whatsoever, especially in close relationships. If your own wounds are not healed it is very easy for those hurt places to get triggered by another's words. This can hijack your emotions and pull you out of your centered place in the Lord. But as you practice your daily meditation, and do your self-compassion, this will bring about healing and will improve your ability to stay grounded and centered in love with Jesus.

> *Your responsibility as a Christ-follower is to respond from a place of love, grace, mercy and understanding.*

People have a tendency to blame others before they pull the plank out of their own eye (Matt. 7:5). If you become offended, or someone you love becomes offended, it's easy to look at what the offender did rather than what is going on within yourself. You must use all of your triggers as red flags to point you to Jesus and ask, "Lord, why did I respond that way?" Allow any offense that rises up within you to challenge what needs to be healed in your heart. Jesus wants to heal and love these areas by bringing them out of the darkness into the light. This brings you to a fuller state of maturity in Him. We should be challenged in some way by something in everyone. I believe you can learn something about yourself from everyone with whom you come in contact, no matter the depth your relationship may be with that person. If you take the humble road and ask the Holy Spirit to show you why you are challenged or offended, you can use this to grow more emotionally mature in Him.

PERSONAL EXERCISE

Now let's walk through a personal exercise. This might help you apply empathy with a current situation, or it will help set you up for success for your next encounter when you "listen to love" someone. It helps to have a partner in the following exercise, but it's not necessary. You can play both roles as the asker and then the responder.

You and a close friend are having a conversation. He or she says (Choose from the following):
1. Wow, I have a lot to accomplish today.
2. I said I was sorry. What else do I have to do?
3. You never listen to anything I'm saying.
4. Why do we have to keep going over the same old thing?
5. I work hard providing for my family and this is the thanks I get?
6. I believe in God and go to church; what do you mean I'm not 'spiritual enough'?
7. No one wants to hang out with me and I don't understand why.
8. I don't care anymore.
9. It's too late for me to accomplish anything.
10. I have never experienced God's love, but I know in my head He loves me.

Now, with whichever number you picked, I want you imagine how you would respond; think about what you would say to your friend. Colossians 4:6 says, "Let your speech always be with grace, seasoned with salt, that you may know how you ought to answer each one."

As you consider your response, remember:

• Don't confuse hearing with listening. You may try to hear everything someone is saying and still miss the meaning.

• Stay focused. This is why your meditation time is such an important tool because it trains the mind to stay focused on the Lord.

• Be centered in your Spirit. Remember to stay in your True Self when listening to others. Your True Self is love-based, which keeps you focused on caring for the other person.

• Listen to their heart; not just the words they are saying, but also the feelings behind the words.

• Learn to accept what the other person is saying without judgment.

• Listen for completeness, such as emotions and relevant information. If incomplete, ask questions for clarity.

• Give feedback of what you think and felt they were saying. Continue to give feedback until you are sure they know they are understood by you.

It always helps to process your thoughts before you engage with someone. This can be done by rehearsing in your mind or writing then down.

Now is a good time to practice your responses. You can jot them down, and then check out some examples of responses in the back of the book in the Appendix to see how you did.

Chapter 7

ALL ABOARD THE BRAIN'S TRAIN OF THOUGHT

*"The intuitive mind is a sacred gift and the rational mind is a faithful servant.
We have created a society that honors the servant and has forgotten the gift."*
– Unknown

Your brain is a very complicated and delicate piece of human machinery that God made, and it's actually more integral and related to your meditation practice and healing process than you may think. Before we move on, I want to share more about some basic brain anatomy and what takes place in your brain as you engage in meditating on Jesus and His word.

In discussing the brain, I want to give you a basic overview just enough so you can get a general idea of the science behind your healing. Since I am not a neuroscientist, I have relied heavily on the published findings of medical journals and Christian neuroscientists' research that ties science and scripture with our brain. This portion will actually help you later in this book as you master learning your love-based truths and how to let God heal your emotional hurts and fear-based thinking.

TWO HEMISPHERES

The largest part of the brain is the cerebrum. This is what most people picture when they think of the human brain. The cerebrum is comprised of two different regions, called hemispheres—and this is what I want to focus on and discuss a little further. But both hemispheres influence your conscious and subconscious mind.

The conscious mind makes up only 10% of the total brain, whereas the subconscious mind makes up 90% and is accessed by the right hemisphere.[32] Think of the conscious mind like the tip of an iceberg; the visible part makes up a very small percentage, while the "unseen" majority represents your subconscious. The left and right hemispheres of your brain each serve unique roles and affect how you process your thoughts that affect both the conscious and subconscious mind.

THE LEFT HEMISPHERE

This is the side of the brain mostly responsible for your thinking. Analysis, logic and reasoning take place predominately in the left hemisphere of the brain. The left side contains the information files that store facts,

---

[32] Peter Scazzero, *Emotionally Healthy Spirituality,* (Grand Rapids: Zondervan, 2006), 15-16.

common to the ones you typically learn in school. The reasoning part of your brain does not start to develop until around the age of three, which is typically when a child starts to ask "why?" in their conversations as they discover and interact with things and people. It's full development peaks around the age of 20.[33]

The portions of the brain most central to mathematical function and speech operate in the left side. With language as a dominant function, words that you think or speak can become stored in your subconscious, but you have the ability to choose or filter which ones can enter. What you allow into your subconscious is what comes out in your behavior.

If you don't choose which thoughts or words you let in, then the thoughts with the most emotional impact and the words you believe will automatically be stored in the subconscious. This is why it is so important to guard the thoughts you allow in to your subconscious because it directly impacts how you live life from the thoughts that take place in your mind.

The goal is to eliminate any negative thinking or false beliefs because it keeps you from God's best. Doing your self-compassion exercise will reveal how much your negative thinking has affected your thought process. This is why scripture commands us to take every thought captive (2 Cor. 10:5) and to "guard your

> *Loving statements have a positive healing affect when spoken or thought upon.*

---

[33] Harry W. Carpenter, *The Genie Within: Your Subconscious Mind*, (Fallbrook: Harry Carpenter Publishing, 2011), 40.

heart above all else, for it determines the course of your life" (Prov. 4:23 NLT).

This left side is the only side of the brain that identifies the passage of time and can function with the flow and order to piece together past-present-future (so it can make sense of an event that takes place). Consequently, this side gives you the ability to plan for the future and use hindsight.

The left brain is prone to repeated loops of cyclical thinking (I like to refer to it as ruminating)—so any kind of thoughts your brain initiates, whether positive or negative, have their circuitry established in the left hemisphere. It is dangerous to worry about a future problem that ruminates with thoughts such as "What if [this] or [that] happens," because the root of your thinking is fear-based and allows negative statements into your subconscious to be stored and then acted upon later. This is why God tells us to not worry about tomorrow "For tomorrow will worry about itself. Each day has enough trouble of its own" (Matt. 6:34).

However, loving statements have a positive healing affect when spoken or thought upon. Your life will take a much different avenue if you choose thoughts such as, "I am loved, valued, and cared for"—which are rooted in truth and love, not fear (John 3:16, Isa. 43:4).

How you compare and judge others is a function that also occurs in the left brain. Since it tends to perceive you as an individual—a unique, separate self, it is considered by psychologists to be the ego-centered part of the brain. This can become a problem, particularly when negative brain chatter occurs and you judge or compare yourself or something or someone. Statements such as, "I'm not any good," "I'm worthless," "I don't measure up," or "I'm not wanted here" are evident of the Ego being central and dominant. This is very important to remember when you are dealing with healing old wounds because you do not want to keep reinforcing negative beliefs.

THE RIGHT HEMISPHERE

This is the part of the brain responsible for feeling. This is what is connected to the subconscious because it communicates with feelings and images. The right hemisphere does not recognize the "I" as a distinct individual like the left brain does; rather it sees the "we"—the relational connectedness. The right side of the brain allows you to feel connected and at one with God, with others and the world.

Creativity, vision and intuition all take place predominately in the right hemisphere of the brain. This side is also responsible for musical and artistic skills. It recognizes patterns and is very competent to perceive things visually and based on feelings or "hunches." The right hemisphere is your intuitive component that connects you to the voice of the Holy Sprit—unlike the left side that computes information with linear, rational thinking. You can simplify by labeling the left brain as "the thinker" and the right brain as "the feeler."

Your right brain is not very good at articulating words; it mainly uses feelings or pictures, as in dreams, visions, or your imagination to describe things and experiences. People who are asked why they love their spouse, or how they know they are "the one" can have difficulty articulating their 'why' into words, because they're engaging their feelings and intuition in their right brain as to how they "just know."

It is important to note that the right hemisphere of our brain does not and cannot perceive the past like the left brain does. All it knows and exists in is "the now." Yet, it gives us our ability to dream and envision our future.

The right brain is the seat of our emotional and social awareness, so feelings (as well as pictures) are sensed and recalled from the right. Empathy and compassion are strengthened here: it's where our imagination exists. I want to emphasize the importance of this: if you want to change your life for the better, then by using your Godly imagination, picture the things the Bible say are true about you:

> See that you are made in the image of God and have value. (Gen. 1:27)

> Picture in your mind how you have been called and have purpose beyond the pain in your life. (Rom. 8:28)

> See your hope and future, despite your current circumstances. (Jer. 29:11)

This not only starts a new pathway in your thought process, but also commands the subconscious to work with the Holy Spirit to accomplish the desired outcome.

Despite each hemisphere being so different from the other, integrating both hemi-spheres is necessary. You need the right hemisphere to feel empathy toward others and your self—to feel connected, to be at peace and to fully experience the present moment. Yet, you also need the left hemisphere to help you interact as distinct individuals in the world. The left hemisphere gives you a sense of self and provides the sense of time, order and sequence that allows you to accomplish tasks. We need both: the left's language, logic and rational thinking skills and the right's emotions and connectedness with God and others.

BE OF ONE MIND

Proverbs 23:7 tells us our heart is connected with our thinking: "As a man thinks in his heart, so is he." But there are times we can sabotage ourselves with double minded thinking when our beliefs do not match up with God's truth. This is where I want to tie in how the mind functions together so you can "be of one mind" (Rom. 15:6).

The first step is having "the thinker" (left brain) agree with "the feeler" (right brain). In this process, there is a part that is sometimes ignored: Do the beliefs held in your subconscious agree or disagree with God's truths within your spirit?

> *If the beliefs you hold in your subconscious are different than what scripture declares, then the unbelieving thoughts will overrule your faith.*

A person's beliefs, or belief systems, are the things a man or woman grows up to understand as perceived truth; it's what got handed down to you culturally and within your own experience of life. If the beliefs you hold in your subconscious are different than what scripture declares, then the (unbelieving) thoughts will overrule your faith:

"But let him ask in faith, with no doubting, for he who doubts is like a wave of the sea driven and tossed by the wind. For let not that man suppose he will receive any-thing from the Lord; he is a double-minded man, unstable in all his ways." (James 1:6-8)

"But be doers of the word, and not hearers only, deceiving yourselves." (James 1:22)

This becomes a crucial component to understand when you begin your healing process, because it helps you keep your thinking positive and in alignment with truths of God's word.

If you say, "I'm hopeless in this situation," then chances are likely you will have no hope because your subconscious is translating your conscious thoughts into real-time actions and obeying that command. Your subconscious mind will take what you say or think literally to try to achieve what has been said. This is how we self sabotage in double-mindedness: when those two things—our belief systems and the word of God—are different or out of alignment.

Have you ever thought, "It's been months since I've dropped or broken any dishes" and then soon after you break something on accident? Whether or not you "knock on wood," it does not jinx you either way; it's your subconscious mind that heard and processed the action to "drop any dishes."

I have had to change my conscious language because I realized the damage I was doing with the words I was either thinking or believing in my mind. I have seen the power the subconscious can have, and I wanted to create only the best outcome for my life. In the past I would say things such as, "I hope I don't get a sinus infection"—and all my sub-conscious could interpret from that statement was, "get a sinus infection." Most likely, and on many occasions, I would. Now I have learned how to only state the positive truth of God's word in "the now" or present tense: "I am staying healthy, healed and have a strong immune system." This thought is based in the truth found in Isaiah 53:5 and 1 Peter 2:24.

When you bring the thinking-conscious left brain together with the feeling-subconscious right brain in alignment with the will of your spirit, you walk in unity with God. The conscious part of your left brain has the will to do something, and the subconscious part of your right brain has the power to do it. This is when the dunamis[34] power of the Holy Spirit is activated. The alignment with God's truth and your beliefs, coupled with faith, is what creates the manifestation of your desire. I must emphasize your heart's desire has to be love-based because perfect love always wants and can satisfy the best for everyone involved, not just what's best for you (1 John 4:7-10). These components of thinking, feeling, belief, and faith in one accord allow you to walk in His power.

> The alignment with God's truth and your beliefs, coupled with faith, is what creates the manifestation of your desire.

HOW THE HEMISPHERES AFFECT YOUR HEALING

The way you interact with the world and how you think about yourself, others and God, is internalized through a patterned network of thinking that gets established

---

[34] Dunamis is the Greek word translated from Strong's Concordance (#1411) referring to "might, power and marvelous works (of God)."

very early in life. Your initial relationships and the input from your surrounding environment are particularly vital in shaping your brain. When infants are born, right brain activity over-shadows and dominates the left-brain circuitry. This is why our earliest childhood experiences carry particularly powerful and long-lasting emotional reactions into adulthood.

Because of this, you develop a set of neural networks—a pre-programed road map that directs your thoughts and emotions—and it ends up affecting you by coloring your world through your childhood experiences. The way you think and behave is encoded into these neural networks of your brain. Because those earlier established ways of thinking tend to get repeated use throughout your life, this is what causes your thinking patterns in your neural circuitry to be strengthened.

TRAUMA

Emotional traumas or hurts impact your brain in significant ways. Hurts and negative feelings from others—especially in childhood—are subconsciously accepted into our neural circuitry as your brain develops. As I mentioned earlier, the higher core-reasoning region of the left side of the brain does not become functional until later in early childhood, around the age of three years old. Since infants and young children are right-brain dominant, the emotionally charged right side is responsible for processing and holding on to any trauma. This means the pathways for processing trauma and holding it in one's memory are hard-wired into the core and right hemisphere regions of the brain.

Since the right side of your brain can only remain in 'the now,' often times you can get stuck by carrying your trauma into adulthood. Whenever you undergo something traumatic, or are subject to any repeated, hurtful events from your past, that memory—complete with sensory detail and emotional content—is subconsciously stored in your circuitry as being significant to your basic survival. A little girl who was sexually molested at an early age can take that traumatic experience into her adult life and become extremely self-protective in her relationships since she had no protector at the time of her molestation. Traumatic events trigger any similar feelings and mannerisms you have whenever you encounter anything similarly in life, later on down the road.

A traumatic experience can be likened to a flash flood. Imagine floodwaters carving a deep channel into the earth; rain from future storms naturally flows and follows the same channel that was originally caused by the storm's floodwaters with each subsequent storm.

> *Any new experience that relates in some way to an old, original trauma has the ability to 'trigger' a person with the same emotional intensity.*

In a similar fashion, a strong neural pathway is established when a 'storm' (trauma) hits the brain. Once a trauma has occurred, it becomes a pathway that is laid down as a default 'channel,' and this pathway tends to be used over and over again to process any later events that are triggered by a comparable experience.

Any new experience that relates in some way to an old, original trauma has the ability to 'trigger' a person with the same emotional intensity he or she originally associated with the first experience, or trauma. In more extreme cases, this incident is referred to as Post Traumatic Stress Disorder, or PTSD.

Although the traumatic of hurtful event was damaging when it first occurred, it is the re-activation of the pathways associated with the event that causes the ongoing pain and hurt. Conscious or subconscious hurtful memories have a profound impact on how we respond in our current situation and how we emotionally react to everyday events in our life.

Let's look at four steps of what takes place during a traumatic incident. When the fight-flight-freeze mechanism is triggered within you, your left side of your brain shuts down in direct proportion to the intensity felt during the incident. Every emotion, visual and physical sensation is funneled over to your right side of your brain.

1. Since the left hemisphere recognizes the passage of time, a time element is not connected to the traumatic event since your right hemisphere has taken full command authority. The right hemisphere operates only in the present moment (the now), thus causing the traumatic incident to get frozen in time or buried alive.

2. With the right brain in control, the left brain cannot function in its role of calming the feelings and physical reactions. This is why you cannot reason with yourself to respond very cool and collected if something has been triggered. It is also why any triggering event causes a similar level of emotional intensity as when the original event took place.

3. Because language is centered in your left brain, your right brain might not make it possible to remember the event consciously with words. Rather, memory for the trauma-induced emotional response is often stored only at your subconscious level in your right brain.

4. Your response to a traumatic event originates in the core area of your brain. Trauma memories are fear-based. Higher level, love-based empathetic responses of compassion and kindness get left out since they are not hardwired into the traumatic memory.

In Daniel Siegel's book, *The Mindful Therapist*, Siegel gives a clear, real life example of what it looks like when trauma memory networks laid down in childhood get reactivated.

This well-known author and child psychiatrist was sitting at the breakfast table one morning when he inadvertently dropped an antibiotic pill on the floor. Before Siegel could stop the family dog, she licked up the pill—or at least that's what Siegel assumed. In a panic, Siegel leaped out of his chair and chased the dog. Wrestling her onto the floor, he pried his dog's mouth open searching for the pill. Even as an MD, he knew logically that a single dose of one antibiotic pill would not hurt the dog, but he still experienced his heart pounding and a cold sweat that broke out on his forehead. Meanwhile, his teenage children continued eating their cereal and calmly pointed out that the pill lay on the floor beside the table leg.

Later that day, Siegel took the time to process the event. He remembered a time when, as a boy, he had sprinkled snail bait in the yard. The next morning he unintentionally let his young dog out into the yard, and the puppy ate the poison and died.

The incident at the breakfast table served as the trigger to set off the same cascade of neural firing patterns established in the original sensitizing event that killed his puppy years ago. His over-reaction at the breakfast table had come as a result of an old channel of network neurons being reactivated.

An unhealed hurt or wound can be readily recognized by the emotional responses it produces. Research has shown that it takes approximately 90 seconds for the initial fight, flight, or freeze response to dissipate. After this brief time, the neurochemical activity of the brain returns to resting levels. If it's an event triggered by an initial (old) wound, it will set off an old pattern of responses. These usually last longer than 90 seconds.

This helps us understand that when someone has an emotional reaction out of proportion to what is warranted by the situation, it gives a clear indication that an old trauma has been reactivated. This is our red-flag indicator that informs us an unresolved hurt or wound still remains and needs to be healed.

> *When someone has an emotional reaction out of proportion to what is warranted by the situation, it gives a clear indication that an old trauma has been reactivated.*

A helpful rule of thumb I personally use is the "3 Minute Rule." An emotional reaction to an event that lasts more than three minutes and is out of proportion to the emotions warranted in the situation indicates an unhealed hurt that has been triggered. This is a place where you must learn to stop and go to God to find out the true cause behind what's triggering you.

It is vitally important you learn to pay attention to your emotions. They speak the language of your soul. By being sensitive to your emotions, you will be able to hear what is going on within you and give yourself the compassion and attention you deserve. Out-of-proportion emotions are the voice of a hurting soul crying out for help: "I don't have the words," the soul declares, "but something is not right; I'm hurting; help!" Recognizing your emotions as indicators is your first step to healing.

King David opened himself to God and prayed, "Search me O God, and know my heart; try me and know my anxieties; and see if there be any wicked way in me, and lead me in the way everlasting" (Ps. 139:23-24). David asked God to search his soul and heal what was not right from within. Even though it may feel or seem scary to face emotions that feel like you're spinning out of control or relinquishing control of your life, God wants to rid you of every anxiety and hurtful emotion you have or will ever encounter. His heart's desire is for you to know and be known as your True Self.

CHANGE IS POSSIBLE

Your thoughts define you as a human being. The word of God says, "For as he thinks in his heart, so is he" (Prov. 23:7). From your thoughts come the actions that make you uniquely you. Science shows us how we think changes the neural circuitry in our brains, and this becomes an important game-changer in how we "set our minds" (Col. 3:2) or focus our attention.

Pornography is one area of weakness I've unfortunately witnessed people suffer in their thought lives. Romans 8:5-6 (NIV) says, "Those who live according to the sinful nature have their minds set on what that nature desires, but those who live in accordance with the Spirit have their minds set on what the Spirit desires. The mind of sinful man is death, but the mind controlled by the Spirit is life and peace."

> From your thoughts come the actions that make you uniquely you.

We can choose to use our thoughts to manifest good or evil actions. When people visually absorb any kind of picture or image, whatever they view is getting stored into their subconscious and will directly impact their future behavior. I believe all of us desire to live a life of freedom and peace, but many times ruminating on what we think is "insignificant" to our walk with God is the very thing that can rob us from a mind controlled by the Spirit.

If the right brain and subconscious work in tandem to file away mental images, and the left brain recycles them like a movie that runs in the background, then we tread on dangerous ground when our thoughts are not holy, pure and honorable to God.

If you are ruminating on pornography, your thoughts are mapping your road to the very act of adultery since your mind is set on images pertaining to that behavior. Harry Carpenter, an expert in the field of the subconscious mind wrote in *The Genie Within: Your Subconscious Mind*, "Your subconscious mind will act to achieve whatever goal it is given whether the goal is well thought out, haphazard, or provided by an outside source."[35]

> *Wherever love-based circuitry is strengthened, fear-based circuitry becomes silenced.*

Since thoughts are directly tied to a person's action, this not only makes adultery equal with pornography in God's sight, it also eventually can lead directly into the physical action of adultery. This is why Jesus tells us in the scripture "Don't think you've pre-served your virtue simply by staying out of bed. Your heart can be corrupted by lust even quicker than your body. Those leering looks you think nobody notices—they also corrupt" (Matt. 5:27-28 MSG)..."And if your right hand entices you to sin, let it go limp and useless! For you're better off losing a part of your body than to have it all thrown into Hell" (Matt. 5:30 TPT).

I hesitated to write about this subject, but due to the overwhelming amount of clients and families I counsel who deal with the destructive and devastating results of this addiction, I felt it necessary to show how this can help be prevented with a deeper awareness.

No matter what you're facing, repairing your brain's circuitry is possible. Neuroplasticity, which is your brain's ability to change, is greatest and has the most capacity in infants and young children. But no matter how much you age, your neural networks are like plastic—they can be reshaped. Clinicians are beginning to use this information to help others rewire their

---

[35] Harry W. Carpenter, *The Genie Within*, 69.

brains and teach people how to change their mind and behavioral patterns.

As Christians, we do this by consciously choosing to think differently by meditating on God's truth. You first have to be aware of what you are actually thinking about. Meditation creates what is referred to as awareness. You know you have reached a higher state of awareness or (as I like to refer to it), God consciousness when you are able to think about your thinking and be mindful of your thoughts on a regular basis.

When you repeatedly focus your attention on something, such as God's love, activated neurons gradually form an established pathway from the new thoughts on which you are meditating. Because of God's design of our brain's neuroplasticity, we can "be transformed by the renewing of our minds" (Rom. 12:2).

Wherever love-based circuitry is strengthened, fear-based circuitry becomes silenced. Depending on what you think about or dwell on, your brain will store emotions that are either toxic or healing in your body.[36] This is why the Bible commands us to take every thought captive:

> For the weapons of our warfare are not carnal but mighty in God for pulling down strongholds, casting down arguments and every high thing that exalts itself against the knowledge of God, bringing every thought into captivity to the

---

[36] Caroline Leaf, *Who Switched Off My Brain: Controlling Toxic Thoughts and Emotions,* (Southlake: Thomas Nelson Publishers, 2007).

obedience of Christ, and being ready to punish all disobedience when your obedience is fulfilled (2 Cor. 10:4-6).

Worshiping Jesus Christ, our God of love, actually stimulates those neural circuits responsible for healing, empathy and compassion for one's self and others. God wonderfully created our brain, so meditating on Him and His truths becomes the perfect answer for our healing. The God who knit us together so perfectly in our mother's womb, has provided a way out—through our God-given ability to connect with Him!

> *Worshipping Jesus Christ actually stimulates your neural circuits responsible for healing.*

LETTING GOD HEAL YOU

You do not have to stay stuck in painful memories and downward spirals of negative thoughts and actions. Sleepless nights of worry, fits of anger or bouts of depression arising from an old, fear-based nature do not have to control you. But you have to make the decision to stay yielded and present with the Lord. Matthew 6:34 (MSG) says, "Give your entire attention to what God is doing right now, and don't get worked up about what may or may not happen tomorrow. God will help you deal with whatever hard things come up when the time comes."

Picturing the True Self in meditation actually helps you to walk in the True Christian Person here on Earth. As you picture yourself daily, standing in your true identity as the True Christian Person, you are rewiring your mind to have a complete change of perception of who you are in Christ because you want to see yourself as Jesus sees you. As you allow Him to renew your mind by rewiring your circuitry with His empathy and love, your lies will be disproved and the healing truth of His word will set you free.

"This I say, therefore, and testify in the Lord, that you should no longer walk as the rest of the Gentiles walk, in the futility of their minds, having their understanding darkened, being alienated from the life of God, because of the ignorance that is in them, because of their blindness of heart. Be renewed in the spirit of your mind, and that you put on the new man which was created according to God, in true righteousness and holiness" (Eph. 4:17-18, 23-24).

Chapter 8

UNCOVERING LIES

"Of all the liars in the world, sometimes the worst are our own fears."
                                                    – Rudyard Kipling

For the longest time I believed I was "the dumb one" in my household. Not only were my family what I considered 'brilliant,' but their perception and treatment toward me reinforced there was no way I could be as smart as them being the only right-brained, left-handed, ADD red-headed one in the house.

Years later, and before I became a counselor, I was given an IQ test in the midst of my banking career that qualified me for specialized training. I was as shocked as were all of my peers to be qualified for the "cream-of-the-crop smart ones" among other chosen colleagues. I had taken on the role of "the dumb one" my entire life to that point. As I became an addiction counselor, I aced my certification with honors, and the Lord ran home His message that He wanted me to see myself as He saw me. These two events began to unravel a lifetime of lies that were built upon lies.

Before you can fully address the hurtful emotions and bring healing to your wounded parts, you have to assess how much damage has been done from the lies you have believed. Lies are something harmfully wired into your neural circuitry, which is why it is so difficult to pin point them—especially if you have grown to believe it is your truth. In order to recognize your own wounds, there are a couple of indicators that help expose a lie that's hidden, based off of what triggers you. These triggers can be good indicators of where to start looking for lies.

Whenever you have repeated exposure to a hurtful experience (such as an ongoing dysfunctional environment) it entrenches all the false beliefs you have about your life and of yourself. Additionally, hurts you experienced early in life are especially prone to develop strong, foundational, subconscious lies that distort the truth about your True Self. The earlier these lies set in, the more they will appear to be 'truths' to you. Some of the depths of these lies may have you completely unaware of what you're believing, and you may need outside help from someone you can trust who not only knows the word of God, but knows the truth of who you are in Christ (such as a counselor or a spiritual advisor).

> *The false beliefs you have accepted about any given situation is what continues to cause you harm in your present-day life.*

Friend, what I want you to recognize is this: it is your perception and interpretation of any traumatic event or incident that causes you emotional damage, more than the incident itself. This is why all emotional pain carries a false belief, or lie, that you must learn to recognize and replace with God's truth.

The false beliefs you have accepted about any given situation is what continues to cause you harm in your present day life. These are what become our "wounds" or what I refer to as a wounding. The enemy—the deceiver of the brethren and the father of lies—uses these false beliefs and your wounds to keep you in bondage to your False Self (John 8:42-47).

When an emotional wound remains unhealed (whether or not you realize it or refuse to deal with the pain of it), the false belief or lie connected to it directly affects your behavior. David Seamands, a pioneer in the field of Christian counseling developed a benchmark, that if a person's reaction to something exceeds the level of attention it warrants and lasts longer than 30 seconds, there is a lie that we've believed at some point in our past. My rule of thumb is if a reaction last longer than three minutes, it is a good indicator there is a lie present because a wound has been triggered.

Your wounds can also affect your physical body. Some scientific research is now coming forward with evidence that confirms this and has proof to help us see how our negative emotions that develop from our thoughts, is transferred into or carried by our body.

According to Luis Diaz, who has pioneered a technique called "Cellular Memory Release," or CMR, Diaz assesses that "unconscious strategies"—lies or false beliefs—"are manifested in a way to match the energy field of repressed fears, traumas and wounds that are stored within the cellular memory."[37] So whatever you come to falsely believe as "true" affects you at a cellular level, which is directly related to how healthy or sick your body is, or can become.

The CMR therapy Ruiz and his colleagues are testing is revealing that when negative emotions and beliefs are released or surrendered in a person, the negative energy also stored at the cellular level is also released, and the emotional and physical healing is finally possible.

This concept was what God showed me years ago as I learned about the power of meditation and how it brought me freedom emotionally, physically and spiritually. Bringing the lies up and out of the subconscious heals the body since the lies have not only been stored in your emotions, but also etched into your cellular memory.

HOW LIES AFFECT YOUR BEHAVIOR

When you believe a distorted version of the truth about yourself, you act in accordance with the lie you believe, rather than the truth of who you are in Christ. It is important to remember you have been given a new heart and a new spirit. Ezekiel 36:26 says, "I will give you a new heart and put a new spirit within you; I will take the heart of stone out of your flesh and give you a heart of flesh."

In an effort to explain and justify what has happened to us during a trauma (whether you were an infant, child

---

[37] Luis Diaz. CMR "The Cellular Memory." April 2016.
http://www.cellularmemory.org/about/about_cellularmemory.html.

or adult) we tend to make up our own story, and this becomes our truth, which actually is a lie.

> *When you believe a distorted version of the truth about yourself, you act in accordance with the lie you believe.*

Accepting a lie gives you the feeling of having some level of control over your world. This gives you a way to cope with the hurt so you can go on living. The lie then becomes your survival mechanism; but it also causes you to subconsciously live in agreement with the fear-based false belief. In order to live in freedom, you must learn to not only confront the lie, but also know the truth of God's word and replace it as your new truth (2 Cor. 10:3-5).

A prayer I call my "3 'R' Therapy" will help you remember how to do this:

1. Recognize the lies;
2. Rebuke the thought connected with it; and
3. Replace it with His truth:

> *"Lord, help me to become aware of the thoughts that bombard my mind. Help me to recognize if these thoughts are speaking truth or lies. If a thought does not line up with Your word Lord, help me to rebuke that thought in the power of Your name. Then Lord, replace that thought with the truth of your word and Your love that flows into my entire being. Amen."*

A young girl, for example, who has been sexually abused, may come to believe an assortment of lies after one or several encounters of being sexually exploited.

Through this horrific atrocity she endured, her brain tries to make sense of the trauma that she cannot explain herself. This is where the lie takes shape.

She may believe, "No one could love me." Or if she believes that she has no value and is worthless, her brain accepts this lie as her own truth to help resolve and cope with why she was abused in the first place. This deep-rooted sense of being fundamentally unlovable—which, by the way, is a potent, toxic lie—can affect her entire life in a variety of destructive ways.

> *Your Ego operates on the lie-based premise that God does not love you.*

In many scenarios the false belief can drive her behavior and define her as a person if she isn't able to identify and confront the lie. This can express itself in her striving to be an over-achiever, or it may develop into sexual promiscuity, perfectionism, or it could push her into any variety of addictions to try and mask the pain. In an effort to continue on and resume normalcy, she will subconsciously act out the best way she knows, in a lifelong attempt to prove herself worthy because of what the incident(s) caused her to believe.

Your Ego operates on the lie-based premise that God does not love you. If you fall prey to believing this, then the Ego determines the behavior of your False Self. In this way, lies form the structure upon which the False Self is built; slowly but surely, your False Self begins to convert the lies you believe into destructive behavior.

If a man working his way up the leadership ladder without understanding and believing the love God has for him, he will continually strive for achievement and approval from those above and around him. Since his value is not rooted in the identity of Christ's love for him, he will fight to prove his worth or value to others, and this can take on various forms of expressed behavior.

He could demand respect from others if he feels he's not getting the respect he thinks he deserves; he could speak ill of a co-worker who is vying for the same upward position, or maybe even lie or twist the truth to defend his position and put the fellow employee in the wrong light. Depending on the depth of the False Self, he can fall into addictions, backstabbing, and deceptions of various forms and levels. Having the false beliefs about his value may even express itself in having a deep need to be right no matter what the cost to others. This behavior exposes his Ego that believes "self protection is more important than the hearts or lives of other people." How many lies he has believed will determine his potential behavior.

We live in a world in which our relationships with God and others are tainted with fear-based lies that war against God's truth. Most of these false beliefs are embedded in our subconscious mind, so it's not easy to recognize, much less replace the false beliefs with the truth of God's word. It is difficult to combat lies with our intellectual mind, even scriptural truths, because these lies have been falsely established as "facts" in our mind. This is why we need the power of God's Holy Spirit (Rom. 8:11).

Although each person's false beliefs may vary, the root of every lie still remains the same, whether we mistakenly believe others don't love us, or we cannot love them, or we don't know how to love ourselves, or that God cannot love us. Fear obstructs God's love

> *The key to getting to the root of a lie or false belief is entering into the subconscious through the Holy Spirit's love.*

toward us, and this affects how we perceive the truth of God's word.

God's truth is love-driven, and love is infinitely stronger than fear: "There is no fear in love, but perfect love casts out fear, because fear involves torment. But he who fears has not been made perfect in love" (1 John 4:18). We know that God has given us a spirit of power, love and a sound mind—not one of fear (2 Tim. 1:7).

The key to getting to the root of a lie or a false belief is entering into the subconscious through the Holy Spirit's love. We use the avenue of meditating on His word to accomplish this: "For the word of God is living and powerful, and sharper than any two-edged sword, piercing even to the division of soul and spirit, and of joints and marrow, and is a discerner of the thoughts and intents of the heart" (Heb. 4:12).

You have to learn the truth of God with your mind, will and emotions and then meditate on them until the new neural pathways are formed with God's truth as your new foundation. God's love-based truth will always override your fear-based lie. Fear is usually a good indicator that something isn't coming from your True Self, but originating from the False Self, or Ego. The deeper your fear and false belief are embedded, the greater your fight.

Maybe you grew up not feeling loved or valued, but as a Christian you know that God's word makes that a lie. You will need the power of His truth to renew your mind, or a war within your thoughts could manifest. This might look like a fear of believing your spouse would leave you, or at the least, that they couldn't possibly love you like he or she says they do. In my practice I see this as a common occurrence. With the discipline of meditating on God's truth and learning self-compassion, it doesn't take long for the mind to be renewed with the inner peace of God's truth to become your new default.

RECEIVING GOD'S LOVE

Allowing God to love you is an ongoing process. God does the loving; your part is only to receive. But receiving isn't as easy as it sounds. Receiving depends on your willingness to come to God as an open vessel and be shaped by Him. Can you discipline yourself to sit quietly each day in His presence? Can you trust Him enough to let Him dismantle the walls of self-protection you have erected because of the fear-based lies? Can you trust Him enough to present yourself to him as a living sacrifice so He can search your heart and prune out poisonous deception?

Even if you answered, "yes" to all of these questions, the Ego within us all has a different agenda. Romans 8:7 tells us "because the carnal mind is enmity against God [...] it is not subject to the law of God, nor indeed can be." Webster's dictionary defines enmity as "warring, hostility, or ill will."[38] It will be a battle to strengthen your True Christian Person against your Ego that wages war and is hostile against your True Self.

---

[38] "Enmity." *Merriam-Webster.com.* 2011. http://www.merriam-webster.com/dictionary/enmity.

Again in Galatians, the Bible tells us the "flesh lusts against the Spirit, and the Spirit against the flesh: and these are contrary the one to the other: so that you cannot do the things that you would" (Gal. 5:17). Without God's Holy Spirit working within you, it is impossible to overcome anything in your own strength (Phil. 4:13).

As you believe more and more of how much God truly does love you, you will come to trust Jesus on much deeper levels. This trust will lead you to desire surrendering your ego-driven, strong-willed, fear-based behavior. This makes surrendering to His loving ways and His perfect will for your life so much easier because now you trust Jesus rather than your old lies. Through His love for you, you will continue your journey of opening yourself up to more of Him. You will cease to think with your carnal mind and instead, begin functioning with "the mind of Christ" (1 Cor. 2:16). Your new way of thinking will take you straight into the destiny He has designed for you.

This battle continues until at some stage in your mature Christian walk, the Ego completely submits to your spirit man so you can continuously walk in your True Self.

In God's design, the soul bends its knee to the Spirit. No longer does the mind hold the false beliefs impressed upon it by the world and your wounded relationships with others. No longer does your Ego lead and drive you. Now, the word of God has renewed you from within and you are ruled by the Spirit. But this is something you must continue to do daily—spending time with Jesus through His word and meditating on Him to remain strong in your spirit man.

We have seen how hurts and traumas affect our developing minds and work their way into our way of being and functioning. We have seen how fear-based lies attach themselves to these hurts, further compounding the problem and keeping us in bondage to the False Self. When difficult times arise, God's word gives us hope to continue this inner journey of healing:

> Therefore, having been justified by faith, we have peace with God through our Lord Jesus Christ, through whom also we have access by faith into this grace in which we stand, and rejoice in hope of the glory of God. And not only that, but we also glory in tribulations, knowing that tribulation produces perseverance, and perseverance, character, and character, hope. Now hope does not disappoint, because the love of God has been poured out in our hearts by the Holy Spirit who was given to us. (Rom. 5:1-5)

Remember this is a courageous journey. The work that I've done in partnering with Jesus to overcome the enemy's lies buried in my life helped me take a 180-degree turn from my despair and co-dependency, into my freedom in Christ. Just like Paul encouraged the believing Christians of his day, I want to encourage you to continue this upward journey toward the call of God that's on your life.

Chapter 9

FINDING THE HIDDEN GIFTS

"It's okay to be a glow stick: sometimes we need to break before we shine."
– Unknown

God's love is your foundation for healing. But there is something even greater to be discovered about His love for you. Behind all your hurt, trauma and lies you've believed, are gifts that have been hidden away. My definition of these special gifts is *any lost or stolen part of your original personality that has been uncovered and redeemed during a healing that has taken place.* These (gifts) arise in the distinctness of who God created you to be. Because of His abundant, rich love for us, God gave you and I precious gifts each embedded in our own personality traits. This can look like anything from a desire for deep intimate relationships, compassion for the hurting, or having a strong ability to lead and take authority.

It took much of the Lord's healing before I could see His gifts He originally placed in me. God took a lifetime of assorted pain and heartache, and restored the years "the locust had eaten" (Joel 2:25) to use for this ministry. God redeemed my gifts to have deep relationships and connect and love others so I could now walk them through their own inner healing.

Your gifts speak of the Lord's divine intentions for your life, which are directly connected with your mission and calling.[39] God created each of us differently and with particular gifts. Your gifts, talents and abilities make you totally different from anyone else in the whole world. This is what sets you apart to uniquely accomplish your own special destiny.

> *Your gifts speak of the Lord's divine intentions for your life.*

I believe if we all knew deep in our heart how important and distinct our purpose is, and why we exist to accomplish that purpose, we would have a more beautiful perspective of this world and a greater excitement for our lives. Ephesians 2:10 (TPT) says, "We have become his poetry, a re-created people that will fulfill the destiny he has given each of us, for we are joined to Jesus, the anointed one. Even before we were born, God planned in advance our destiny, and the good works we would do to fulfill it!"

Since the enemy knows this, he tries to destroy the work of God in you by taking your God-given gifts and using them to derail your purpose. Satan wants to take

---

[39] Caroline Leaf. *The Gift in You.* (Southlake: Inprov, 2009), loc 33.

your *strengths* of personality and turn them into areas of *weakness* that predispose you to sin, and at minimum, distract or discourage you from your future. The evil one's desire is to turn your gifts "inside out" and use them for his sinful purposes to steal, kill, or destroy them completely.

The good news is that Christ has won this battle over Satan, and God's plan and purpose will prevail. In John 10:10, Jesus says, "The thief does not come except to steal, and to kill, and to destroy. I have come that they may have life, and that they may have it more abundantly." Part of that abundant life comes from redeeming your gifts that get turned inside out.

HALLWAY OF THE HEART

If you can imagine a part of your secret place having a long hallway with doors on both sides—this is what I refer to as "the hallway of your heart." Each door leads to a room that contains a 'gift' yet to be opened. Allowing the Lord to redeem your gifts is like receiving and embracing every gift behind each door in your heart that has been locked away by your protective Ego. If the enemy can deceive you into believing nothing good could come from behind these closed doors, your Ego will continue to keep you from freedom and healing.

> *The enemy tries to destroy the work of God in you by taking your God-given gifts and using them to derail your purpose.*

In this hallway of your heart, picture each room representing a painful area in your life. We all consciously or subconsciously tuck away memories we don't want revealed or don't want Jesus to examine because our Ego has believed any number of the enemy's lies. Either way, the Lord desires for you to open the doors that may be painful or traumatic, because behind each door lies freedom, healing, gifting, and restoration from what the enemy has tried to destroy. The love of Jesus you experience in your meditation will allow you to continually grow in your trust of Him, and this trust will empower you to go to the hurtful, painful places in your heart. Only then you can release His deep healing to begin. This is your safe, sacred place you and Jesus will visit often as you do your healing work.

DISCOVERING YOUR GIFTS

Let's learn how to discover your precious gifts. Since your gifts have been given to assist your purpose in life, it is helpful to begin looking at your basic God-given character traits.

Remember: among your spiritual gifts, there are other gifts that are hidden behind every wound and every sin. To uncover these treasures, it is helpful to ask:

❑   "Is there a hidden gift behind an offense that was committed against me?"
and

❑   "What is the basic character trait that predisposed me to act out with unhealthy behavior?"

Suppose a young man is coerced by his peers and breaks into a house with some friends. In this instance of his decision to sin, he was easily talked into doing something wrong in order to gain acceptance from his peers. Even if it caused him to act illegally by breaking and entering, he sought acceptance by a group of people over breaking the law. If his gift remains unredeemed, he will seek to please *people*, rather than God. When redeemed, his true gift is a compliant nature of obedience to his Lord and having a servant's heart that desires to help others.

Similarly, a woman looking for love in all the wrong places may discover that her unique gift is a desire for deep intimacy with God. Her gift is that she was wired to have deep intimacy with Jesus as her bridegroom— not a relationship addiction found in other men, a boyfriend or even her husband.

A man addicted to pornography might find his hidden gift is actually finding his worth in Christ alone. Or it could be God has given him a deep desire for an intimate loving relationship. His gift turned inside out may be a root of anger and control toward women, and that desire became skewed early in life by another's inappropriate behavior either around him or towards him.

When someone inherently hurts you in a sinful way, the enemy tries to thwart the expression of your gift. In the case of the young man who broke into the house, he may have suffered from abandonment from his family of origin, which left him longing to belong. With the woman looking for love, she may have never felt accepted, valued or approved of by a close male relative. With the man addicted to pornography, he may have experienced an inherent disrespect from a person who carried the matriarchal role in his family. These hurtful wounds could be so concealed that they may be unperceivable unless revealed by the Holy Spirit. If someone sinned against you, it would be helpful to ask, "What was the gift that allowed me to survive that hurtful time?" and, "What was the character trait that developed as a result of that trauma?"

> *When someone inherently hurts you in a sinful way, the enemy tries to thwart the expression of your gift.*

Finding and reclaiming your gifts turned "inside out" is a critical step in the journey to wholeness. As you learn about how to do a healing on the wounded parts of you, it may be difficult to discern what your gift is that got turned inside out. If you have trouble with this, take heart; your dilemma most likely stems from using your left, logical side of your brain to find your gift.

Your left hemisphere works primarily to reason what your gift could be, trying to figure out what it is instead of consulting the Holy Spirit first. The right brain is the intuitive side that will give you the prophetic insight to help you understand and know what your gift truly is. This prophetic insight is developed through your meditation time and whenever you do your self-compassion, encouragement and surrender throughout the day. This is why I am such a strong advocate of making your meditation and self-compassion a daily and consistent practice: the more you do your meditation, the stronger your prophetic gift will become.

If you get stuck and don't know what your gift is, I have found it to be the perfect opportunity to ask the Holy Spirit to reveal your gift to you. Whether or not you receive a clear answer right away, you will have more and more clarity with time and practice.

Based on the healings I've done and helped walked other people through, I've developed a brief list of what people's gifts can look like when redeemed.

This is not a hard and fast list, so you must continue being sensitive to the Holy Spirit's leading in order to have confidence of which gifts are for you (since they may defer from this list) whenever you walk through a healing.

GIFTS INSIDE-OUT   REDEEMED GIFT(S)

GIFTS INSIDE-OUT		REDEEMED GIFT(S)
Abandonment	→	Loyalty, acceptance, love, reliance on God
Rejection	→	Encourager, compassion, mercy
Shame	→	Encourager, empathy, love, acceptance, humility
Humiliation	→	Forgiveness, peace, mercy, empathy
Anxiety	→	Peace, faith, freedom, joy, boldness
Betrayal	→	Loyalty, discernment

It is worth exploring your hidden gifts in spite of the fear you may experience from facing the wounds triggered within you. Confronting the anticipated pain and discomfort of whatever has been buried so deep in your heart will unlock the freedom that gets hidden by your self-protective Ego.

Redemption and freedom are part of your legacy: "knowing that from the Lord you will receive the reward of the inheritance; for you serve the Lord Christ" (Col. 3:24).

TWO BECOME A WHOLE ONE

Gifts you receive are precious and vital. Once the Holy Spirit helps you redeem your gift, your gift and the newly healed part of you that was once wounded becomes joined together. This brings you into wholeness from the broken (wounded) parts that were once shut off and buried from the Lord.

> *It is worth exploring your hidden gifts in spite of the fear you may experience from facing the wounds triggered within you.*

Ephesians 2:14, 15-16 says, "For He Himself is our peace, who has made both one, and has broken down the middle wall of separation [...] so as to create in Himself one new man from the two, thus making peace, and that He might reconcile them both to God in one body through the cross, thereby putting to death the enmity." This scripture originally speaks to the prejudice wall between the Jews and Gentiles, but in context to the False Self and True Christian Person, it can relate to bringing your False Self that experienced wounding, and incorporating it into your True Self who is one with Christ. The merging of these two establishes your healing with total wholeness and oneness with Jesus.

Discovering your lost gifts allows you to see how the enemy caused you to have a distorted self-image from the lies you have believed: "Now, if anyone is enfolded into Christ, he has become an entirely new creation. All that is related to the old order has vanished. Behold, everything is fresh and new" (2 Cor. 5:17 TPT). Uncovering your gift reclaims the lost part of you and reconciles it back to God.

God's definition of healing and wholeness is beyond our comprehension. First Thessalonians 5:23 (MSG) says, "May God himself, the God who makes holy and whole, make you holy and whole, put you together—spirit, soul and body—and keep you fit for the coming of our Master, Jesus Christ."

You cannot be the person God created you to be and walk completely healed and whole, without embracing your gifts as part of your unique personality. As I look back and see all the gifts that God has redeemed in me, I stand in awe of the magnificence of my Lord. He took all of my anger and control issues that were turned inside out and transfused it into my spirit to fuel my internal burning flame of passion for the call He placed upon my life. I feel like an arrow that has been shot from His quiver, soaring through the air to my destination with Him.

The next and final step to this journey of living free is to walk through a healing, so you can integrate all God has entrusted to you for your purpose and destiny. I will teach you the basic steps where the Holy Spirit can show you what needs His healing touch, and how to reach your greatest potential in Christ.

Chapter 10

HEALING, RESTORATION & REDEMPTION

"The day misspent, the love misplaced, has inside it the seed of redemption. Nothing is exempt from resurrection." – Kay Ryan

Up to this point, you've learned how to experience the Lord's unconditional love for you, and by loving your human self the same way, with compassion and kindness, you have built a strong foundation to begin an even deeper walk with God. As you've explored gifts turned "inside out," you have all the pieces needed for healing. All we have to do now is to put those pieces together.

Over the years of helping others to heal, I have seen consistency in how God works to set us free. The following is not a method that must be followed; rather, it is a suggestion for how to proceed. I have found this to be very effective in helping others along the healing path over my 25 years of experience. When you walk through these steps, it will look different for every person. I share this to shed light on a beautiful, highly creative and individual process that only the Holy Spirit can orchestrate in you.

When I first walked myself through a healing, I had trouble wanting to face what woundings existed. But then the Lord showed me an inner desperation that wanted and needed His perfect love. The Lord had to teach me and guide me through this whole process of doing an inner healing. Even as we fumble through our best efforts, it is the Spirit of Jesus that does the work, so don't worry about "getting it right." Rest assured this is an incredible healing experience that is personally yours.

Begin by starting your meditation by going into the secret place. You want to find a relaxing and undisturbed place where you can focus to go from your head down into your heart (reference Chapter 3 for the steps outlined on meditation).

Start by seeing yourself as your True Christian Person. You must first envision your True Self because it establishes the grounding of who you are in Christ; *this is very important because it serves as the emotional safety net for your healing.* Without this, it is easy to re-enter the wounding and the old pain, or get lost in the disorienting, lie-based thought patterns of the wounded part. This is a critical key for self-protection. If you cannot see your True Christian Person, then picture your human self. This automatically places you into your True Self with ease.

As you begin to meditate, work your way down the stairs, across the courtyard and into the secret place within you where you commune with Jesus.

Ask the Holy Spirit to show you the image of yourself that has the wounding and/or holds the false belief. Let the Holy Spirit show you (as the True Christian Person) an image of yourself at that age. Wait for what is revealed to you.

As your True Self, ask the wounded part if (he/she) knew Jesus at the age of the wounding. If (he/she) does, then continue. If (he/she) doesn't, then stop and explain who He is and let the wounded self trust and embrace Jesus and His Lordship. Then have Jesus ask to adopt (him/her) into His family. If (he/she) is not ready, ask what would (he/she) need from Jesus in order to enter into His family. I have usually found what the wounded self needs is as simple as an assurance that Jesus won't ever leave or forsake that part that experienced hurt (Heb. 13:5).

Allow your True Christian Person to reassure the wounded part (he/she) is loved and treasured, making sure to speak kind and comforting words. Console the wounded part that it is not (his/her) fault that (he/she) believed a lie. Tell (him/her) that your True Christian Person is so sorry for the hurt (he/she) has carried all these years. This uses your self-compassion in the situation.

Take some time to establish a heart connection whereby the True Christian Person loves that wounded part; allow the wounded part to accept the love being given. The True Self may need to ask the wounded part for forgiveness of neglect for not being there or aware of all the hurt. ("Would you please forgive me for not being there for you during [that hurtful time]?") The wounded self may have tolerated much negative self-talk up to this point, which is what I refer to as negative thought abuse. Asking forgiveness is necessary because it replaces your inner critic's self-hate with love from the spirit-filled True Self that only Jesus gives.

Once the wounded part feels safe with the True Christian Person, ask the wounded part about the false belief by clarifying the depth and extent of the wounding. Ask: what is the wounded part feeling? What does (he/she) believe about (him/herself)? Why does (he/she) feel that way? This will help you determine the lie that came with the wounding. You may continue to ask these questions to help get to the bottom of the wounded part in you.

Comfort the wounded part and reassure (him/her) that it was not (his/her) fault for believing the lie. The wounded part did the best (he/she) could during that traumatic event. This strengthens your roots of self-compassion.

Gently ask the wounded part if there is anything else to share or reveal with you. Let the True Christian Person respond with empathy.

Allow Jesus to dialog also. What compassionate words does Jesus want to speak to the wounded part? How has He come to heal? What promises does He give the wounded part? These promises should line up with God's word. If the wounded part doesn't hear anything, then quote God's word of what Jesus would say.

Have the True Self verify and reassure the wounded part of the truth and power of Jesus' words.

How is the wounded part feeling now? If the wounded part is safe and satisfied, then continue. If not, help the wounded part feel valuable and loved. The wounded part may have experienced something very traumatic, and it is normal to take a while for (him/her) to trust again.

Ask if the wounded part has anyone (he/she) needs to forgive. If the wounded part has forgiven everyone who has been involved in the wound, then move on. If the wounded part still needs to forgive someone, this is the time to do it. Trusting Jesus as (his/her) advocate to bring about justice, let the wounded part tell Jesus (he/she) forgives the person (or people) and release the offender to Jesus to avenge any wrongdoing.

Next comes discovering your redeemed gift; ask Jesus to reveal the gift that has been turned inside out. Thank the wounded part for carrying the gift. Tell the wounded part that you cannot step into your destiny without (him/her) and the gift (he/she) holds.

Ask the wounded part if (he/she) wants to live in your heart as part of the True Christian Person with you and Jesus. This is where the redemptive restoration is completed. If the wounded part is not ready, ask what (he/she) needs, either from the True Christian Person or Jesus. Scriptures such as Deuteronomy 31:6 and John 15:4 will affirm trust from Jesus to the wounded part.

Let your True Self hug and embrace the wounded part and hold (him/her) close. Imagine the reunion in your mind. See the wounded part melting into the True Christian Person. This now joins the wounded part with your True Self.

Once the pain is gone, peace pervades. You can revel in the wholeness and beauty of the healing that has just taken place. Thank Jesus for the healing, your restoration and redeeming your gift.

There is no need to rush this process. Let the Lord do His work completely and thoroughly throughout the healing. Sit quietly to absorb what the Lord has done for you. Finish by recording it electronically or hand-write in your journal what the Lord has just completed.

Let the Spirit of Jesus give you the words and feelings; following the prompting of the Holy Spirit is beautiful and good. Make sure to allow God's forgiveness, mercy and love to flow freely between your True Christian Person and the wounded part of yourself.

Sometimes, my clients have gotten stuck in determining what their wounding is. You'll know what the wound is as you answer questions that clarify more about your trigger: why the anger (or other emotion)? What about it hurt the most? How did it make me feel about myself? When you get to the bottom of the lie you believed, you will encounter the painful emotion (sadness, anger, a sense of loss, etc.) and discover the wound. At that point, you can walk through the rest of the healing steps mentioned above.

If you are afraid in any way to approach what might need healed in your heart, you must remember the Lord will not enter in unless you invite Him in: "Look at me. I stand at the door. I knock. If you hear me call *and open the door*, I'll come right in and sit down to supper with you (Rev 3:20-21 MSG, *emphasis added*)." In this healing process, the Holy Spirit will always honor the individual. A healing cannot be forced upon the wounded part; let God do it in His way and timing.

DOING PHYSICAL HEALING

If you have a physical ailment or disease in your body, this step-by-step process of restoration and healing prayer can also be replicated for physical healing, just as much as it does for emotional healing. The one difference you must keep in mind is to continually pray over the physically sick part if you do not receive immediate healing in one sitting.

> *A physically or emotionally ill part may want to give up because it can grow so weary of fighting.*

I like to picture a separate recovery room where Jesus stays by the sick person's side until healing takes place. The True Christian Person can step in to pray over that sick person until he or she is healed. Do not integrate that part until he or she is completely healthy; keep going back to pray over him or her when you meditate. I've seen this work for clients who have faced and overcome many long-term ailments and trauma disorders.

There are going to be times in your life when you find yourself tired of struggling or fighting with an ongoing situation. A chronic issue can be emotionally and/or physically draining if it feels too hard to deal with or face. Depression, addiction, anxiety, illness, PTSD and high levels of stress at work or at home are all examples where this can happen.

A lack of breakthrough in any of these areas can make anyone feel very discouraged, so it is important you remember to do your self-compassion exercises throughout the day, every day. No matter our spiritual or emotional maturity, we can all ignore or neglect part of ourselves that needs love the most.

A physically or emotionally ill part may want to give up because it can grow so weary of fighting. Self-compassion from the True Christian Person, who is one with Jesus, will release the healing power from the Holy Spirit directly into the part in need.

At the same time, it frees your body of the negative energy that has been stored in your cellular memory. This healing may or may not happen instantaneously, but you will experience its fruit as you continue to practice your ongoing healing prayer. Our God is a faithful God.

We know that our Lord wants to set us free: "Let me be clear, the Anointed One has set us free—not partially, but completely and wonderfully free! We must always cherish this truth and stubbornly refuse to go back into the bondage of our past" (Gal 5:1 TPT). Be encouraged and remember God is a God of process and this inward journey to healing and wholeness is a process of becoming more Christ-like and growing in His image.

SETTING CAPTIVES FREE

The focus so far has been on the way God wants to love and heal *you*. The emphasis has been getting you to personally surrender and trust in the love of God, so hurtful emotions and fear-based lies will no longer fill your mind and drive your behaviors. However, the story doesn't end here. Your healing, wholeness and freedom is not the end of the road. In a way, it only marks the start of the journey.

Jesus called into the tomb, "Lazarus, come forth" (John 11:43) and the man came forth alive, up and out of a grave. But when Lazarus stepped out from the tomb, he was still bound up in grave clothes. He was alive, but he looked dead. So Jesus told the onlookers, "Loose him and let him go" (John 11:44b).

Jesus raised Lazarus from the dead, but He did *not* unwrap Lazarus from the grave clothes; others among the crowd did. God has given us the awesome privilege of participating with Him in the joyful task of freeing not only ourselves, but also others.

Once you experience some measure of freedom from the hurts and lies you previously believed—and you begin walking in the truth of God's great love for you—love and truth will radiate from you. You will find yourself responding with genuine empathy and compassion to others who are hurting. You will become a vessel of His

> *When you take responsibility for your healing and step up to help others, the Body of Christ can advance together in freedom.*

love, grace, mercy and healing and you will begin to be used by God to set others free. This is God's design. Scripture tells us, "For you have been called to live in freedom, my brothers and sisters. But don't use your freedom to satisfy your sinful nature. Instead, use your freedom to serve one another in love" (Gal 5:13 NLT).

We do not have to be completely healed of all our own wounds to participate in this work because God wants us to participate in helping others. All we need is to have God's love for others, an understanding of how God works to heal and a willingness to be used to help set the captives free (Luke 4:18).

Using the basic understanding of the True Christian Person as your foundation, you remain in Christ and hold the testimony of how God has worked in your life to free you of hurts and lies; these are essential tools for freeing others. Our True Self naturally wants to love others and set them free to become their True Self, too. The powerful God-truths that worked in your life are the same God-truths that will work in the lives of others.

When you take responsibility for your healing and step up to help others, the Body of Christ can advance together into freedom. Christians shall rise from the dust of emotional hurts and false beliefs and become a powerful, united force for good on this earth—what an encouraging mission and purpose we have! We cannot do it alone: "Two people are better off than one, for they can help each other succeed. If one person falls, the other can reach out and help. But someone who falls alone is in real trouble" (Eccl 4:9-10 NLT). No matter how healed we think we are, we have never "arrived." We need others and others need us. God made us that way—to be relational and interdependent human beings.

We desperately need fellowship; not only with God, but also with other believers. Picture an army of warriors, healed and whole, marching together in battle array, freeing captives who then join the army. Their capacity to live and fight the good fight of faith against the enemy is exponentially doubled when they are empowered to live freely and walk in wholeness. This is the heart of our Lord Jesus, and it is my passion as a counselor and founder of the Live Free Healing Ministry:

> The Spirit of the Lord is upon me, and he has anointed me to be hope for the poor, freedom for the brokenhearted, and new eyes for the blind, and to preach to prisoners, 'You are set free!' I have come to share the message of Jubilee, for the time of God's great acceptance has begun. (Luke 4:18-19 TPT)

> *It is possible to walk with God fully healed and whole on a daily and continual basis, while you're on Earth.*

God will make it clear who is ready, or desperate even, to become healed and whole. Then in gentleness and love—with genuinely caring—it becomes your privilege to help others down the path. You cannot force this. Accepting people where they are in their process in their own spiritual journey will usher in a way for you to show compassion and unconditional love, which empowers them to come to you. It might be helpful to share this book with a person you know. If he or she is ready, introducing Christian meditation might be more beneficial; or, you might feel led to lead the person in healing a wound. Every situation will be different, but the Holy Spirit will lead you down the right path as you look for His direction.

One day a friend of mine and I were talking over coffee. She began sharing how she *hated* a part of herself for being molested as a young child. I asked, "Why do you hate that part?" and my friend explained how she viewed it as weak and (therefore) disliked weak people.

As I discovered more about her situation, she said she felt weak because at the time it happened, she didn't tell anyone about being molested. When I asked her why she didn't say anything, she responded, "My parent's lives were already in turmoil; I didn't want to add another burden."

When she said this, it became clear that her true gift was being a protector. She sacrificed herself for those she loved; she acted to guard her parents from further hurt. Although the gift turned inside out resulted in unhealthy silence, the gift was right there underneath it all.

With her permission, I had my friend close her eyes and embrace the image of herself as the person who God made her to be. Once she could get an image of her True Christian Person, I asked her to see the wounded part of herself from that period of time of the incident. Then, I asked to have her True Self tell the wounded part how proud she was of that (wounded) part for being so strong in her self-sacrifice* and protecting her parents, and how she regretted not being able to accept and love that aspect of herself until now.

When my friend imagined embracing the young, broken part of her, a new love and respect for that wounded part emerged and she was able to welcome and integrate that aspect into herself. With her eyes still closed, I asked her what the gift might be redeemed, and she saw it: God made her to be a protector. Revelation of her true gift came to her as powerful insight.

My friend was astounded at the transformation that had taken place within; self-hate had instantly departed. God's love for that hurting part had come in. She actually felt proud and grateful for the gift the Lord had given her. My friend walked away feeling stronger, freer and more confident as a woman of God.

The gift Jesus initially instilled within her had now been joined as part of her True Christian Person. More of her life started conforming to the truth of God's love— and to my amazement, all of this occurred while sitting outside of a local coffee shop. This true story illustrates the simplicity of healing and how readily it can be used to help others and how powerfully God works! Her healing may not yet be complete—but until we deal with all of our woundings and keep our Ego out of the way, neither is yours nor mine. God wants you to walk fully healed and whole with Him on a daily and continual basis, and *this is possible* while you're here on Earth.

By staying in His presence and by learning to enter into the place of our inner man or woman where the Lord continually dwells, we learn how to live out of our True Selves. In that sacred place, our Ego has no power over us because it has fully submitted and surrendered to the guiding of the Holy Spirit. It's in this place where we abide in divine, unbroken union with Jesus.

Once you confront your wounds and have them healed, it's only a matter of staying out of your Ego and in your True Self that you have complete freedom and wholeness before you get to Heaven. This is when you face a difficult situation or an offensive person in your life, but can respond with the love of Jesus because you're resting and responding from your True Self—not reacting out of your ego-centric, False Self.

> *You were fashioned to be in constant fellowship with God, to meditate on Him, to be loved by Him.*

After you've gone through all your healings, you may encounter what feels like a wound. Since dying to the False Self (Ego) can feel like deep emotional grieving, do not be fooled; this is how the "dying to self" process may feel.

God designed us with minds that would rest in Him. We were fashioned to be in constant fellowship with God, to meditate on Him, to be loved by Him. As you worship Jesus as the One who so loved the world with the greatest love, your mind will be transformed (John 3:16, Rom 12:2). Those around you will be affected by how you reflect the love of Christ, and will be challenged to change as they see Jesus in you.

This requires us to walk in our true identity, which is what God wants for us. He doesn't just want you healed enough so you feel better on this earth. He wants you to become all that He created you to be, that you may be filled with all the fullness of God (Ephesians 3:19).

We each have a book written in heaven about us. It tells of the True Christian Person God created in us: "Your eyes saw my substance, being yet unformed. And in Your book they all were written. The days fashioned for me when as yet there were none of them" (Psalm 139:16). What is written in your book? Your Lord wants the fullness of who you are in Christ to come forth.

In His death upon the cross, Jesus has accomplished everything for us to become the True Christian Person that He intends—and this is great news: "The One who called you is completely dependable. If he said it, he'll do it!" (1 Thes 5:24 MSG).

Appendix

EAR Exercise: IT'S ALL IN THE EAR[40]

As good listeners, it is important to always have an *ear* for the one speaking. Using this as an acronym, "EAR" stands for Empathy, Attention, and Respect. This gives us a simple reminder of our role as compassionate listeners.

> Empathy creates the heart connection between listener and speaker.
> Attention makes the person feel validated.
> Respect gives the speaker the feeling of acceptance.

Empathy creates the heart connection that is soothing and calming and lowers any intensity that might be present. For example, you can show empathy by saying something such as, "I can see how important this is to you," or "I understand how this process can be frustrating." It is NOT saying to a person, "At least you don't have it as bad as the next guy," or "You know, you should at least really be grateful for the more important things in life."

Attention lets the speaker know that you are interested in them as a person, giving them permission to continue. This can happen, for example, by saying something such as, "I will listen as carefully as I can," or "I am interested in what's going on."

Respect encourages and makes the speaker feel safe so they can continue to become more open and vulnerable. This allows the Holy Spirit to open their heart to the deeper emotions. Examples of respecting someone can include expressions such as, "I can see that you are a hard worker," or "I respect your persevering in this difficult time."

All three together have a powerful effect on the person who is entrusting you with their heart, because your quality and depth of connection with people hinges on EAR—and with discipline, will develop trustworthiness in your relationships.

---

[40] THE E.A.R. Exercise , Bill Eddy, LCSW, Esq.@2011 By High Conflict Institute

I am *Statements:* WHO I AM AFTER THE CROSS

This list supplements chapter 2's "I am Statements," along with the counterparts (wrong/opposite responses) to God's truth.

I am Statements	Wrong / Opposite Responses
I am blessed, bestowed upon (Deut. 28:6)	Relies on self-empowerment; based on works or achievements
I am chosen, set aside for purpose (John 15:16)	Compares; life has no meaning or purpose; depression
I am holy, Christ-like (Eph. 1:4)	Striving, performance, self-sanctification
I am blameless, pure (Heb. 10:22)	JERD (Justify, Explain, Rationalize, and Defend)
I am love, adored (Eph. 2:4)	Acts of service, negativity, very needy
I am adopted, handpicked (Rom. 8:15)	Not special, ordinary, no purpose
I am washed, pure (1 Cor. 6:11)	Shame-based; walks with guilt and blames others
I am accepted, approved (Rom. 8:7)	A continual need to prove oneself to others; often feels "one-down" or talks to others in a "one-down" attitude (teaching or giving advice). Often feels rejected or like a nobody.
I am redeemed, paid in full (Gal. 3:13)	Unworthy; often feels they don't matter, count or have any value
I am forgiven, debts cancelled, acquitted (Heb. 8:12, Eph. 1:7)	Strives to be good; self-rejecting/hate
I am anointed, consecrated, chosen, by divine intervention (Deut. 28:6)	No power to minister; no motivation
I am adorned, enhanced with God's glory (1 Pet. 2:9)	Unbalanced; focuses on one extreme, either not caring at all about appearance, or complete vanity
I am beautiful, feels fearfully and wonderfully made (Ps. 139:14)	Lacks self-confidence or motivation
I am the Bride of the King of Kings (Isa. 54:5)	Incomplete; feels half-empty. Has to get worth from spouse, close friends, family or other people. Never measures up.

Answers to Questions FROM CHAPTER 6

Here is a list of some samples of responses to help you listen to love others:

1. It sounds like you might be feeling overwhelmed?

2. I know you did and I appreciate that. I want to know if you understand why I am upset?

3. I am so sorry you feel that I don't listen. Please let me know in the future when you don't feel heard by me.

4. It feels that way to me also, I would like to find out where we are getting stuck and why this keeps happening.

5. I am so sorry you don't feel appreciated. I value your efforts and will focus on letting you know how much they mean to me in the future.

6. I didn't mean to make it sound like I was judging you. Forgive me if that is how you felt. I appreciate all you are doing.

7. That must feel so lonely, can you share more about what is going on with you.

8. This sounds like you have lost all hope.

9. That sounds like you feel God is through using you?

10. Knowing in your head is the first step, so you can be proud of yourself for that. God wants you to experience His love as much as you want it.

Bibliography and Suggested Reading

Avila, Theresa. *Interior Castle*. Edited by E. Allison Peers. Translated by E. Allison Peers. New York: Image Books DoubleDay, 1961.

Bible Hub. *Strong's Concordance* . http://biblehub.com/greek/1411.htm (accessed August 27, 2016).

Carpenter, Harry W. *The genie within: Your subconscious mind*. Fallbrook: Harry Carpenter Publishing , 2011.

Cleansing Streams Ministries. *Cleansing Streams Workbook*. 2003.

Cloud, Henry and Townsend, John. *Boundaries: When to say yes, how to say no to take control of your life*. Grand Rapids: Zondervan, 1992.

—. *Safe people: How to find relationships that are good for you and avoid those that aren't*. Grand Rapids: Zondervan, 1995.

Diaz, Luis. *CMR*. http://www.cellularmemory.org/about/about_cellularmemory.html (accessed April 2016).

Eddy, Bill. *High Conflict Institute*. 2001. http://highconflictinstitute.com/calming-upset-people-with-e-a-r.

Goll, James. *The lost art of practicing His presence*. Shippensburg: Destiny Image Christian Publishers, 2006.

Got Questions Ministries. *GotQuestions.org*. www.gotquestions.org/rhema-word.html. (accessed August 27, 2016).

Guyon, Jeanne. *Intimacy with Christ*. Jacksonville: The SeedSowers. 2001.

—. *Experiencing the depths of Jesus Christ*. Vol. 2. Gardiner: Christian Books. 1975.

Jennings, Timothy, R. *The God-shaped brain: How changing your view of God transforms your life*. Downers Grove: InterVarsity Press, 2013.

Kübler-Ross, Elisabeth and Kessler, David. *Life lessons: Two experts on death & dying teach us about mysteries of life & living*. New York: Scribner, 2000.

Keating, Thomas. *Invitation to love: The way of Christian contemplation*. New York: The Continuum, 1998.

—. *Open mind, open heart*. 20th Edition. New York: The Continuum International Publishing Group, Inc., 2009.

Kraft, Charles H. *Deep wounds deep healing*. Minneapolis: Chosen books,

1993.

Leaf, Caroline. *Switch on your brain: The key to peak happiness, thinking and health.* Grand Rapids: BakerBooks, 2013.

— . *The gift in you.* Southlake: Inprov, 2009.

— . *Who switched off my brain: Controlling toxic thoughts and emotions.* Southlake: Thomas Nelson Publishers, 2007.

Mehrabian's communication research. *BusinessBalls.* http://www.businessballs.com/mehrabiancommunications.htm (accessed August 27, 2016).

Nee, Watchman, ed. *The spiritual man.* 3 vols. New York: Christian Fellowship Publishers, Inc., 1968.

Neff, Kristin. *Self-Compassion: The proven power of being kind to yourself.* New York: HarperCollins Publishers, 2011.

Sac, David. *Pysch Central.* 28 August 2015. http://blogs.psychcentral.com/addiction-recovery/2012/03/empathy.

Sandford, John and Paula. *Healing the wounded spirit.* Tulsa: Victory House, Inc., 1985.

Scazzero, Peter. *Emotionally healthy spirituality.* Grand Rapids: Zondervan, 2006.

Siegel, Daniel J. *Mindsight: The new science of personal transformation.* New York: Batnam Books, 2011.

— . *The mindful therapist: A clinician's guide to mindsight and neural integration.* New York: W. W. Norton & Company, 2010.

Sorge, Bob. *The secrets of the secret place.* 11th printing. Grandview: Oasis House, 2011.

Stevens, Robert Tennyson. *Conscious language: The logos of now, the discovery, code and upgrade of our new conscious human operating system.* Ashville: Mastery Systems, 2007.

— . *Sacred body language translations: Understanding your body's unspoken language.* Mills River: Mastery Systems Multimedia, 1998-2006.

Taylor, Jill Bolte. *My stroke of insight: A brain scientist's personal journey.* New York: Plume, 2006.

The Nonverbal Group. *"How Much Communication is really nonverbal?"* http://www.nonverbalgroup.com/2011/08/how-much-of-communication-is-really-nonverbal. (accessed August 27, 2016).

Wigglesworth, Cindy. *SQ21: The twenty-one skills of spiritual intelligence.* New York: SelectBooks, Inc., 2012.